W9-AGD-782

Origins
A History Of Canada
Teacher's Guide

Fred McFadden

Fitzhenry & Whiteside

Origins: A History of Canada

Teacher's Guide

© 1990 Fitzhenry & Whiteside

195 Allstate Parkway, Markham, Ontario L3R 4T8

No part of this publication may be reproduced in any form, including any storage or retrieval system, or by any means, electronic, mechanical, photographic, or recoding, unless otherwise indicated, without permission in writing from the publisher.

Author   Fred McFadden
Editor   Dorothy Salusbury
Design   Darrell McCalla
Typesetting   Jay Tee Graphics
Printed and bound in Canada

Origins : a history of Canada
Based on the TVOntario series, Origins.
Includes index.
ISBN 0-88902-450-2

Writers   Denise Boiteau
        Donald Quinlan
        Pauline Quinlan
        Gillian Stuart-Lyon

Consultants   Don Bogle
        Sheldon Diamond

General Editor   Fred McFadden

Editor   Frank English

Graphics Editor   Dorothy Salusbury

Canadian Cataloguing in Publication Data

McFadden, Fred, 1928-
   Origins. Teacher's guide

Supplement to: Origins: a history of Canada.
ISBN 0-88902-452-9

1. Canada – History – To 1763 (New France) – Study and teaching. 2. Canada – History – 1763-1867 – Study and teaching. 3. Canada – History – 1867-1914 – Study and teaching. I. Title.

FC170.0742 1990   971   C90-093289-9
F1027.0742 1990

Origins is published in association with TVOntario and complements the television series *Origins: A History of Canada* by Denise Boiteau and David Stansfield.

Special thanks to the students in class 8-G and their teacher, Ron Fletcher, at Dr. Marion Hilliard Senior School in Scarborough, Ontario, for their assistance in this teacher's guide.

Introduction

Origins: A History of Canada is a scholarly, well-illustrated history of Canada covering the period of Canadian history from the earliest settlements of the Native Peoples, until the significant historical events of the year 1885. It is a survey text which examines all of the major themes of Canadian history during that period. Illustrated throughout in full-colour, it includes many pictures and graphics published for the first time in a Canadian textbook. It is organized into accessible modules or topics, each with varied and related pedagogical activities.

Origins: A History of Canada

Table of Contents

Chapter 1
1. The Beginnings
2. Beringia: The Land Bridge
3. Migration through North America
4. The Origins of Humans
5. The Native Peoples

Chapter 2
1. The Environment
2. The Inuit
3. Before European Contact
4. Spiritual Beliefs
5. Native Communications

Chapter 3
1. Native Government
2. Farming
3. Mayas and Aztecs
4. Trade
5. Disease

Chapter 4
1. The Viking Explorations
2. First Viking Settlements
3. The Brendan Voyage
4. Exploration by Sea
5. Italian Merchant Traders

Chapter 5
1. The Pope Divides the World
2. Decline of English and Portuguese Interest in Newfoundland
3. Fishing
4. Age of Exploration
5. The Europeans Meet the Native Peoples

Chapter 6
1. Cartier Discovers the St. Lawrence
2. Cartier's Contacts with the Native Peoples
3. Cartier's First Canadian Winter
4. Cartier's Third Voyage, 1541
5. Fool's Gold

Chapter 7
1. Effects of Religious Wars on French Exploration
2. Religion in the Americas
3. First English Claim in the Americas
4. A Quest for the Northwest Passage
5. Whaling

Chapter 8
1. The Search for Fur
2. Port Royal — A French Foothold
3. The Beaver
4. Champlain — Father of New France
5. Clash of Empires — English and Dutch

Chapter 9
1. New England
2. New France — A Tiny Population
3. New France — The Vast Empire
4. The Church in the Wilderness
5. Displacement of the Native Peoples

Chapter 10
1. War among the Native Peoples
2. The Iroquois Offensive
3. The Sun King and New France
4. Radisson and Groseilliers: Under Two Flags
5. The French Drive into the Interior

Chapter 11
1. European Wars
2. North American Wars
3. D'Iberville: New France's Greatest Warrior
4. Louisiana
5. Fortress Louisbourg

Chapter 12
1. The Great War for Empire
2. 1740's — The War Continues
3. The Seven Years War Begins
4. Expulsion of the Acadians
5. The Fall of New France, 1759

Chapter 13
1. Quebec in the 1760's
2. "No Taxation Without Representation"
3. Conflict over the Ohio Valley
4. Divided Opinions in the Thirteen Colonies
5. The Loyalists

Chapter 14
1. Causes of the War of 1812
2. The War of 1812
3. The Northwest Company vs the Bay
4. Struggle for the West
5. Struggle for the Pacific Coast

Chapter 15
1. The Great Migration
2. Impact of the Great Migration
3. Unrest in Upper and Lower Canada
4. Rebellions of 1837
5. Emergence of British Columbia

Chapter 16
1. The American Civil War as a Cause of Confederation
2. Internal Factors Leading to Confederation
3. Expansion from Sea to Sea
4. Metis Grievances, 1880
5. 1885: Triumph and Tragedy

Features of *Origins*

Origins is a new history of Canada emphasizing the settlement and early development of our country, with special attention to the story of Canada's original peoples, culminating in the completion of the CPR in 1885.

Origins is a unique textbook:
- Correlated to the outstanding television series ORIGINS: A History of Canada, developed by TVOntario
- Full-colour throughout
- In-depth coverage of Canada's Native Peoples
- Shows relationship of global events to developments in Canada and North America
- Organized into short thematic modules

TITLE/CHAPTER

16 units, spanning the first inhabitants of Canada some 25 000 years ago to the completion of the CPR in 1885.

Chapter One	**A New World**	(23 000 - 9000 BC)
Chapter Two	**The First Nations**	(9000 - 500 BC)
Chapter Three	**Lost Civilizations**	(500 BC - AD 1500)
Chapter Four	**The First Europeans**	(1000 - 1497)
Chapter Five	**The Treasure Hunt**	(1497 - 1534)
Chapter Six	**The Key to Canada**	(1534 - 1543)
Chapter Seven	**God and Mammon**	(1543 - 1583)
Chapter Eight	**Partners in Trade**	(1583 - 1609)
Chapter Nine	**Displaced Persons**	(1609 - 1642)
Chapter Ten	**Empire Building**	(1642 - 1682)
Chapter Eleven	**Balance of Power**	(1682 - 1713)
Chapter Twelve	**The Fall of New France**	(1713 - 1760)
Chapter Thirteen	**The Parting of the Ways**	(1760 - 1791)
Chapter Fourteen	**Struggle for Survival**	(1791 - 1815)
Chapter Fifteen	**Growing Pains**	(1815 - 1858)
Chapter Sixteen	**Forming A Nation**	(1858 - 1885)

INTRODUCTION

Examines major issues to be raised in the unit.

KEY QUESTION

Focusses student attention on the key question for the unit.

CONSIDER THIS

Questions related to the students' own experience, to increase student interest and motivation in the unit.

CHAPTER FOURTEEN / STRUGGLE FOR SURVIVAL

3. The North West Company vs the Bay

In the War of 1812, Canada struggled for survival with the United States in Upper and Lower Canada. It was an area roughly covering today's southern Ontario and southern Quebec. However, around 1800, to the west of this region another struggle was going on. The two rival groups in the West were each based in British North America itself.

What was the struggle going on in Western Canada around 1800?

Consider this
Suppose you were setting off on a canoe trip of 3000 km across unexplored areas of Canada. Describe the kind of leader you would want; the supplies you would need; what perils and problems you might expect to meet.

The North West Company, 1776
Following the British conquest of New France in 1760, many English-speaking immigrants arrived in Montreal. Some of these adventurous new colonists were businessmen of Scottish ancestry. They were men such as James McGill, Simon McTavish, and William McGillivray. They were later joined by Alexander Mackenzie, Simon Fraser, and the Welsh adventurer, David Thompson. Under the new British régime in Canada, these men took over the French-Canadian fur-trading business. The take-over included an army of "voyageurs".

To begin with, these new Montrealers, together with their French-Canadian partners, formed several small separate companies. By the late 1770s, however, they saw the economic advantages of working together. Therefore, they banded together to form one large organization: The North West Company. Thus, the Nor'westers — as they were called

— inherited the entire New France fur-trading network. This was based on the St. Lawrence River and Great Lakes. However, it stretched as far west as the Saskatchewan River.

Nor'westers travelled from a base in the Montreal area as far west as the Saskatchewan River.

272

NARRATIVE

Carefully adapted from the scripts of the TVOntario series by a team of consultants to meet the language needs of intermediate students.

Rationale

Origins: A History of Canada is an outstanding text for the study of Canadian history. It is also unique — it can be used in conjunction with a series of videotapes on Canadian history.

T.V. Ontario developed a series of sixteen one-half hour videotapes in 1988, called *Origins: A History of Canada*. Each half-hour program is divided into five modules examining a particular concept, topic, or question in Canadian history.

The text *Origins: A History of Canada*, was designed so that its chapter organization co-relates directly with the sixteen video programs. Each chapter is divided into five units related to the separate video modules. As a result, Origins is an innovative learning resource for the study of

Origins is organized into sixteen chapters, each presenting five single concepts, for a total of eighty teaching units. Each concept or module is presented over four-to-six pages of text. The units can be followed in chronological order or teachers may choose to focus on selected themes. Each independent topic is accompanied by extensive pedagogical support, including recall and discussion questions, and research and creative activities to develop cognitive, communications, and group work skills.

Origins is a beautifully designed and richly illustrated text with paintings and photographs collected from across Canada, as well as original colour maps and charts.

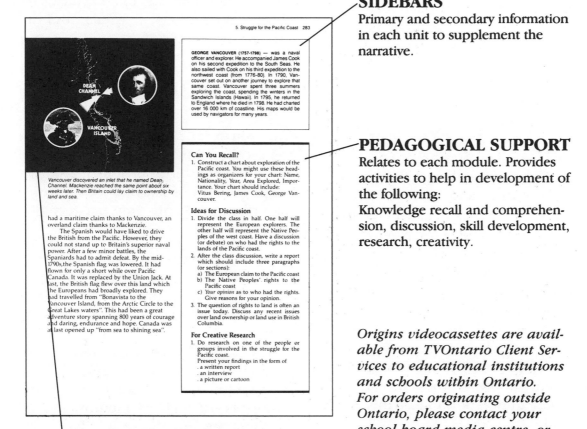

SIDEBARS
Primary and secondary information in each unit to supplement the narrative.

PEDAGOGICAL SUPPORT
Relates to each module. Provides activities to help in development of the following:
Knowledge recall and comprehension, discussion, skill development, research, creativity.

Origins videocassettes are available from TVOntario Client Services to educational institutions and schools within Ontario. For orders originating outside Ontario, please contact your school board media centre, or TVOntario Marketing Division.
2180 Yonge St.
Box 200, Stn. Q
Toronto, Ontario
M4T 2T1

FULL-COLOUR GRAPHICS
Some directly from the TVO series. Includes paintings, photographs, artifacts, documents, maps, and graphs.

Canadian history — a textbook examining 80 topics or concepts, each one supported by colourful, interesting, and dynamic video.

Teachers and students have sought outstanding colourful narrative history books, supported by appropriate, concise educational video resources. For the first time, their requests have been met. This unique package of learning materials provides a stimulating and challenging source for students to learn about our origins and some of the key developments in Canadian history.

Written — in a challenging but attractive style to appeal to students

Organized — each topic or module is organized in a two, four, or six page spread. Each module is a complete learning unit, with narrative text, related graphics, and appropriate skill development and other pedagogical activities.

Large headings — focus students' attention on the key concept or topic; subheadings assist students in organizing the information.

Introduction and Key Question — At the beginning of each topic is an introductory statement, which co-relates with the narrative at the beginning of each section of the video series. The introduction provides background information for students, to help them to understand the issues involved in the module.

This is followed by a Key Question. Too often students see history as an endless series of facts to be remembered, rather than as a series of questions to be explored and answered. The Key Question helps to focus the student's attention on what is pertinent in the following section.

Consider This — raises questions that are to be examined by the students *before* studying the section. The questions raised are to be considered from the student's own experience, and then related to the historical event. It is expected that the student will have greater motivation to study the topic, and have greater understanding of the issues involved.

Narrative text — has been written in an accessible language style to assist student's understanding. The information is based on the video program *Origins*, but has been modified to make the information more appropriate for students. Additional information has been added to provide greater depth of understanding.

Illustrations and Graphics — are in full colour throughout the text. They have been carefully selected to support the written text. Many of the maps, charts, and diagrams have been adapted from the video program. The excellent co-relation of written and graphic materials should enhance the interest and understanding of Canadian history.

Sidebars — of enrichment materials are provided in all units. The supplementary information includes biographical data, diaries, documents, journals, and other primary resources.

Pedagogical — activities are included in each module. They cover a wide range of suggestions for different learning strategies.

Can you recall? — These questions relate to the recall of information in the unit. Although the recall of information is the simplest form of learning, *no* learning can take place without some mastery of information.

Ideas for Discussion — The discussion activities challenge students to apply higher level thinking to more complex questions and issues. Students are required to interpret, to compare, to apply, to analyze, to consider value questions, and to form opinions with supporting evidence. Through discussion, students see that the study of history is *not* just the memorization of information, but that it involves the examination of complex issues and questions. When students are required to form opinions and defend them with supporting evidence, they become *participants* in the events of history.

In many cases, students are asked to compare historical events with current events. In the process, these discussions can lead students to see the relationship of past and present, and to see history as a living subject, rather than the study of the remote and detached past.

Skill development — activities are included in many of the discussion and research activities. Students are required to develop the various communication skills (writing, reading, listening, discussing), research skills, cognitive thinking skills, and group work skills.

Creative activities — are provided to challenge student imagination and innovation. Students may be required to apply their historical knowledge in a creative manner, including interviews, oral presentations, newspaper reports, diaries, group presentations, graphics, and illustrations.

Research activities — are provided for most modules. No textbook can or should attempt to provide all of the information available on a given topic. Therefore, for each topic, appropriate research activities are provided. Students should have the opportunity and the requirement to seek additional information. In so doing, students will not only learn information, but also learn the skills of *acquiring* other information. Thus students will acquire the various skills of research:

— of *selecting or forming* an inquiry question
— of *collecting* data from a variety of sources
— of *synthesizing* this data
— of *developing* a *rough draft* for a report
— of *assessing and editing* this material
— of preparing a *final draft* in finished copy
— of *presenting* the material in an appropriate written or oral manner

The Use of the Textbook with Videotapes

The ideal use of *Origins: A History of Canada* is in conjunction with the videotapes.

Advantages of the Videotape

1. A picture is worth a thousand words — and an appropriate moving picture is even more useful. Most teachers and students have often wished for an appropriate, brief, moving picture to illustrate important and often difficult historical concepts. The video series provides that opportunity.

2. Videos or moving pictures are the medium of communication with which students are most familiar.

3. Short video presentations usually provide sufficient information to introduce the topic in an interesting manner, while leaving time for meaningful discussion, analysis, and related activities.

4. Video has a vocal narrative with sound effects to reinforce the understanding of attractive visual images.

5. Videos and motion pictures appeal to the feelings and emotions of the student, increasing motivation and understanding.

Advantages of the Textbook

However, video has weaknesses and limitations. Most of these can be overcome by using a text in conjunction with the video images.

1. The video, in many cases, cannot be re-examined by individual students to clear up misunderstandings. Although it is possible to replay the video, in many cases logistics will prohibit this. Thus video can be ephemeral with limited possibilities for review and repetition.

2. The video, in most cases, cannot be taken home by the student for individual study.

3. The video often leaves an emotional impression. In most cases, factual information needs to be re-inforced by the printed word. The textbook is often more useful as a subject of rational analysis.

4. The video is an excellent resource, but the study of history and the other social sciences will continue to rely on the skills of comprehension and communication of the printed word.

Origins: A History of Canada provides a unique opportunity to combine the richness, the colour, and emotional appeal of the video, with the comprehension and skill development of the printed text.

Suggestions for Using the Textbook with the Video

Teachers and students can use the textbook and videos in a number of ways according to their imagination and experience. Following is a suggestion of one model.

1. **Introduction** The teacher should introduce the topic in the context of the course (see introduction in each topic or unit in the text)

2. **View** the video (each of these are approximately six or seven minutes long)

3. **Discuss** with the students their comments, reactions, and questions, including an attempt to answer the key question raised by the narrator in the introduction.

4 **Assign** students to complete the *Can You Recall* questions in the pedagogical section, using the textbook as a referral.

5. **Conduct** a class or small group discussion about questions or issues raised in the *Ideas for Discussion* section.

6. **Research**
Where appropriate, assign students *one* or more of the research questions provided. Give the students *specific* instructions regarding length, format, and style. You should also inform students about your expectations and criteria of evaluation for research activities.

You will probably have additional topics for research according to your students and your own interests.

7. **Creative activities** Each student should have an opportunity to participate in a creative activity. Again, you will probably have your own ideas for the creative activities that are effective with your students.

Arrange for deadlines and provide your criteria for evaluation. Plan for selected presentation of some students' activities. It is not necessary for all students to present all of their activities; but over the course of the term or year, all students should have this opportunity.

> *Note — the choice of different activities and the choice of the means of communication (oral report, written, graphic presentation, interview, etc.) gives students an opportunity to* individualize their program. *This choice enables students to pursue their own interests and to demonstrate their strengths.*

8. **Reviewing the video** In many cases it will be appropriate to have some or all students review the video. Often students will gain new insights or meaning the second time around. In many cases, this might be appropriate for individual or small group viewing.

Suggestions for Using the Text Without the Video

1. Teacher introduces the topic. The teacher should explain or introduce the topic in the setting of the course. (See the introduction for each topic or unit in the text.)

2. Consider This

This section provides an issue or question based upon the experience of the student, but related to the historical topic or concept. Have the students react to the topic. The exchange of ideas will relate the students to the topic or concept to be studied, help to motivate them, and assist in their understanding.

3. Read the section on the topic

Students should read the section (2, 4 or 6 pages)

4. Discuss

Discuss with students their reactions, questions, and comments. Ask students to raise any questions resulting from reading the section. Refer to the *'Ideas for Discussion'* questions at the end of each topic. Use these as a basis for discussion.

5. Can You Recall

Assign all students to complete the questions or activities in this section. (You may have additional questions or activities).

6. Research

Assign students *one* or *more* of the research questions provided. Give specific instructions to the students regarding length, format, style, and expected time of completion. In addition, inform students about your own expectations and criteria of evaluation for research activities. You may have additional topics for research to supplement those included in the text.

7. Creative Activities

After research and discussion activities have been completed, assign each student a creative activity. Again, you may have your own suggestions for additional creative activities.

Arrange for specific deadlines and criteria of evaluation. Plan for selected presentations of some students' activities. It is probably not desirable to have all students present their activities each time; but over the course of the term, it is important that all students have opportunities to present some of their material.

Skill Development

The history program should help students to learn and understand important knowledge and concepts in Canadian history. It is equally important that students acquire certain skills. These skills fall into four major areas:
1. **Communication Skills**
2. **Research Skills**
3. **Thinking Skills**
4. **Group or Social Skills**

Suggestions for the Introduction and Development of Skills

1. The teacher should select the time and order of introducing skills. They should be introduced at the appropriate stage of development of students, and reflect their needs.

2. Skills should be taught and introduced in *sequence*, from simple to complex.

3. Skills must be taught explicitly as part of the program. You should not assume that students have already learned a specific skill in a previous grade. In all cases it must be reviewed; in most cases the skill must be taught.

4. Skills in history should be taught in the context of the history program. You cannot assume that because students are learning how to write paragraphs in a language program, that there is an automatic transfer to writing in history.

5. Skills must be taught and repeated to reinforce the mastery of the skill. It is often disappointing to teach a skill and then assume that the student has internalized the skill. Like all skills, there must be repetition to guarantee student learning.

7. Skills, as well as knowledge, should be evaluated to encourage mastery by the student.

Following is a list of skills that can be developed using *Origins: A History of Canada*. (These are explained later in greater detail.) These skills should be integrated into your program at an appropriate time in your student's development. They are listed with simple basic skills at the beginning, and moving towards more complex skills. However, you, the teacher, must decide the appropriate time for introduction. This will vary according to the age, experience, and level of your students' ability.

1. Making notes in point form
2. Recording information in paragraph form
3. Map making
4. Creative writing — journals, diaries, letters
5. Constructing a time line
6. Writing a newspaper account
7. Making an oral report
8. Group work
9. Writing a five-paragraph report
10. Research
11. Problem solving — Cognitive-skill development
12. Writing a research report or essay

These instructions for student skill development may be reproduced or made available to students who are developing a particular skill.

11

1. Making Notes in Point Form

Students should develop the ability to make notes in point form to summarize information from reading the text, or supplementary text, or for research activities. Since it is a basic skill, students should have experience in learning this skill early in the term.

Suggestions for Students
Read the assigned reading to get an overview of the main idea.

Selecting a Heading for Your Note
Sometimes your reading will have an appropriate sub-heading that you can use for your note. In other cases, select the key idea in the reading. Summarize this reading into a few words for your heading. Write or print this heading clearly on your page.

Recording Supporting Statements or Points
— read the selection to find the important supporting statements for your heading
— indent 4 to 6 cm from the left side of the page to create a margin
— record each supporting idea, in brief point form
— start each new point on a separate line
— leave a space or spaces between each separate note

Use this system of summarizing your reading in point form for any occasion in which you want to keep a summary or record of what you have read.

2. Recording Information in Paragraph Form

One of the skills that you will develop this year is the ability to express yourself in your own words in sentence and paragraph form. The first essential skill is learning how to write paragraphs.

A paragraph is a collection of sentences which describe or explain one topic or idea.

A paragraph usually includes an *introductory sentence* which describes the main idea of the paragraph, *supporting statements* to explain the main idea, and a *conclusion or summary statement*.

Suggestions for Writing a Paragraph

1. **Introductory Sentence**
Write your first sentence as a general statement that expresses the main idea of the paragraph.
2. **Supporting Statements**
In a separate sentence for each, write several (three to five) sentences that provide additional facts to expand upon or support your introductory statement.
3. **Concluding Statements**
Write a summarizing sentence that explains why the key idea is important or significant. (i.e. it answers the question 'So what?')

3. Map-making

Guidelines for Drawing Maps

1. Trace the boundaries and coastlines in pencil.
2. When completed, go over boundaries in ink or coloured pencil.
3. Show all coastlines in any identifiable colour
4. Use colour for *meaning*, as well as for making a map attractive. Shade countries in different colours to show their location.
5. Label all important places and features by *printing* legibly, and horizontally (where possible).
6. Print a *title* in a prominent location (at the top or bottom).
7. Where appropriate, use a *legend* to explain the use of colour on your map.

Your task
The Environment (p. 26-31)
Draw a map of North America showing the six major environmental areas. Label each area. Make a legend to show the name of each region.

4. Creative Writing

Many successful history writers use their imaginations to re-create past events. Their work is based on extensive research. After collecting as much information as possible, they use their imaginations to tell the story of past events in as realistic and interesting a manner as possible.

Some examples of creative writing are diaries, letters, and journals. These record facts but also provide writers with an opportunity to use their imaginations. Remember, you must research the information as accurately as possible before writing in a creative manner.

Your task
After using your text and other sources, write one of the following:
Chapter 1, Unit 1 (p. 9)
Imagine that you are hunting a ....
Chapter 1, Unit 5 (p. 25)
Write an imaginary *day-in-the-life* of a native person
Chapter 7, Unit 1 (p. 71)
Write an imaginative description in the style of the Icelandic sagas, of one of the Viking voyages to the Americas.

5. Constructing a Time Line

As a student of history, you will gradually develop a sense of time or chronology. It is important to show *when* things happened. This is not just to memorize unimportant dates; you should know the *sequence* of events, because frequently one event *causes* a later event.

You should develop the skill of placing events in a sequence, and seeing how and if one event affected or caused a following event.

Your task (p. 82-141)
The period from 1490 to 1550 was an important time of exploration of the Americas by Europeans.
1. Construct a time line for the period

   1480 1490 1500 1510 1520 1530 1540 1550
   _____

2. In a small group, select what you think were the most important events of exploration within those years.
3. Locate each event by writing the year and name of the person on the time line in the appropriate place.
4. Below your time line, write the date and a brief explanation.
   i.e. 1492 — Columbus discovered and landed in the islands of the West Indies.

6. Writing a Newspaper Account

The newspaper is one of our main sources of information for understanding world events. A useful form of writing is to describe a historical incident as if you were a reporter at the time of the event.
When you write a newspaper report, you should:
* research and collect the necessary information
* describe the events as accurately as possible, without bias or prejudice
* answer the five ''W'' questions:
  — who? — what? — when? — where? — why?

Your task
1. Read several newspaper reports to see how reporters/journalists write.
2. *Newspaper Account*
   After you have read several news reports, become a reporter and write a story about one of the following events (or choose a topic of your own):
   — The deportation of the Acadians
   — The fall of Quebec, 1759
   — The arrival of the Loyalists in Nova Scotia or Quebec
   — The Selkirk settlement, 1812
   — The completion of the C.P.R.
   — The trial of Louis Riel

7. Making an Oral Report

The ability to express yourself clearly by talking is an essential skill. When we listen to the radio or watch television, we see how important it is to be able to express ideas clearly and in an interesting manner. It is equally important to communicate clearly when we are with friends, or in a class, or when we are working.

In your history class, you will have opportunities to:
* discuss events in small groups
* make oral reports to the rest of your class
* make oral reports based upon your research
* participate in interviews and panel discussions

Your task
You are to prepare a brief oral presentation for other members of your class.

Preparation
1. After you have selected your topic, research to find out information about the topic.
2. Organize your material in a sequence of information that will be interesting to your listeners.

3. Prepare an introduction about your topic that will raise a question or issue of interest your listeners.
4. Prepare a conclusion to sum up the importance of your topic.
5. Write your speech out on *small cards on one side only*. You do not want to have large pieces of paper to distract your audience.
6. Write in point form. *You do not want to read your speech.* You want to express the information in an interesting and dynamic form; people who read speeches tend to lose expression and become dull.
7. *Delivery of Your Speech*
   Think of an announcer or speaker whom you admire, and talk using some of that person's style.
8. Look at your audience as much as possible.
9. You should *refer* to the information on the cards, but should *not* read your speech.

8. Group Work

In many school activities, students learn *from* the teacher or *from* a textbook. As citizens at work, in sports, or at home, we often learn by working *with* other people. In fact, most citizens learn from their friends and associates rather than from a teacher.

Your task

To work in a group with three or four other students, to prepare a *folder of materials* on a given topic.

Procedure

1. Select your topic (or arrange with your teacher for another appropriate topic).
2. Divide the work among your group, so that each person is responsible for completing part of the group task.
3. Conduct your research on your activity. Consult other members of your group for advice and assistance.
4. Arrange to share your reports informally with each other. You should *edit* each other's work before preparing a final draft.
5. When the work has the approval of the other group members, prepare a final draft in the most effective form.
6. When your group has completed its task, prepare a cover for your folder.
7. As a group, plan what could be the most appropriate or effective means of communicating the information to others:
   — brief oral reports
   — overhead transparencies
   — panel presentation
   — rehearsed interviews
   — skit or dramatic presentation

Your task — a group activity — the Viking explorations, approximately 1000 A.D.

Prepare a folder including the following materials:

1. a *drawing* of a Viking ship
2. a *map* showing the route of explorations and North American landings by Vikings
3. a *written note* describing their voyages and their importance
4. an imaginary Icelandic *saga* describing a voyage of exploration on a Viking ship
5. one other activity of your choice.

When you have completed the folder, prepare an appropriate cover for your material.

Evaluation of Group Activity

Your group activity may be evaluated in several ways:

1. Teacher Assigned Mark for Group

	Out Of	Teacher Mark for Group	Group's Self-Evaluation
Organization of Material	3		
Appropriateness of contents	3		
Accuracy and Completeness of Information	3		
Quality of Written and Graphic Material	3		
Effectiveness of Presentation to Rest of Class	3		
Total	15		

2. Peer Evaluation
Students in the group assign themselves a mark as a group.

3. *Groups Assigns Mark to Each Individual*

Within the Group	Out of	Student Mark
Contribution to Planning	3	
Contribution to Research	3	
Contribution to Preparation of Material	3	
Contribution to Presentation	3	
Overall Co-operation Within the Group	3	
TOTAL	15	

Total Mark of Group Activity

Teacher Mark	— Out of 15	_____
Group Mark	— Out of 15	_____
Individual Mark	— Out of 15	_____
	Total 45	_____

9. Writing a Five-Paragraph Report

Writing a five-paragraph report is an expansion of how you write a five-sentence paragraph.

Writing a Paragraph	Writing a Five-Paragraph Report
1. *Introductory sentence* explains main idea of paragraph.	1. *Introductory paragraph* explains main idea of report.
2. *Contents* — 3 or 4 sentences support the introductory sentence.	2. *3 or 4 supporting paragraphs* — Each paragraph explains one idea supporting the introductory paragraph.
3. *Concluding sentence* summarizes or gives the importance of the paragraph.	3. *Concluding paragraph* gives conclusion or significance of the topic.

A common method of communicating your ideas is in a brief report of several paragraphs. These reports should always be written using proper sentence and paragraph form. Each paragraph should be about *one* aspect or part of the overall topic.

Your report should always include:

1. *an introductory paragraph* — this should explain the main idea of your topic.
2. *several supporting paragraphs* — each paragraph should explain, in detail, one part of the overall topic (the number of paragraphs will vary according to the length of your report).
3. *a concluding paragraph* — this will state your opinion about the importance or significance of the topic.

Your task

Write a five paragraph report on Samuel de Champlain — ''The Father of New France''. Write your report in five paragraphs. Following are some suggestions for paragraph topics:

Paragraph 1 — Champlain's overall importance in the exploration of Canada

Paragraph 2 — Champlain as an explorer

Paragraph 3 — Champlain and the fur trade

Paragraph 4 — Champlain as founder of the first settlement at Quebec

Paragraph 5 — Conclusion: the overall importance of Champlain to New France

10. Research

No textbook can provide all of the information required for the study of history. To have a complete understanding of any topic, it will be necessary to do further research in other texts, encyclopedias, and other sources. The following suggestions are offered to assist you in your research:

1. Read your textbook coverage of the subject to gain general background on the topic. This will also help you to begin to *focus* on the questions that you want to pursue in your research.
2. Consult further information sources in your library.
   a) Use the *card catalogue* to help you find other specific books.
   b) Many topics that you wish to research will be only *chapters or sections* of books on a larger topic. Consult your teacher or librarian for assistance in locating these other reference books.
3. Use the *Table of Contents* and *Index:*
   a) When you examine a book, look over the Table of Contents at the beginning. You may determine which chapters are most useful for your further research.
   b) The Index at the back of the book is the most effective way of seeing whether or not the book has information specifically related to your topic.
4. *Recording Information*
   When you find information that you think is worthwhile, record it in point form on your note paper or on 7.5 cm × 12.5 cm research cards:
   — use only *one side* of the page;
   — record information in *point form*, under appropriate headings;
   — record each topic on a separate piece of paper or cards.
   As you record separate topics on separate pieces of paper, it will help you in *organizing* your report when you start to write it.

5. *Bibliography*
   When you complete your written report, you will have to indicate the *sources* of your information. For each book you consult and find useful, record the information in the following way:

Author   Title   City of Publication Publisher Year
(last name (under-
first)   lined)

McFadden, F.C. Canada in the Twentieth Century, Toronto, Fitzhenry & Whiteside Ltd., 1989.

6. When you have collected all of your data or information, you should *organize* your material into an acceptable order. It will help your organization if you have recorded different information on separate pages or cards.

Your Task
Select any topic from this chapter of study, and do further research in the library, using at least two other sources of information.

After completing your research, write a report approximately two pages long.

11. Problem Solving — (Cognitive-skill Development

We live in a very complex world that is often difficult to understand. We are often dependent on the newspaper and T.V. journalists for our information and our opinions.

As independent citizens, we should be able to inquire into problems to help form our *own* opinions. This involves our ability to:
— *examine* information
— *focus* attention or raise questions
— *organize* information into an interpretation or theory
— *research* for additional information
— *analyze* our data to modify our ideas
— *communicate* our ideas to others in writing or orally

When you can manage these skills, you are on the road to becoming an independent thinker.

Your task

To construct a *chart*, using inquiry skills on the topic: *Immigration to Canada between 1815 and 1860*

This is a very large topic. Therefore, you should be narrowing your study on one aspect of the topic, such as: *Problems faced by immigrants in the period 1815 to 1860.*

Method

1. *Focus your research*
   — What problems did immigrants have in Britain and Ireland in this period?
   — What problems did they have in getting to British North America?
   — What problems did they have in establishing a homestead?
   — What problems did they have in making a living?
   — What social, religious or educational problems did they have?
   — What other problems might they have had?
2 *Organize*
   As you do your research, use the questions as *organizers* to collect your research.

Type of problem	Problem
Problems in Homeland	
Transportation	
Land Settlement	
Financial	
Social	
Political	
Other	

Collect your data under these headings as you read and do your research.

3. *Locate more information*
   You will usually find that your textbook does not have enough information to answer these questions. Using the school or public library, consult additional books to find further information.
4. *Recording your information*
   As you do your research, record the information under the headings that you have provided; e.g. Transportation
5. *Communicating your information*
   There is little value in learning information unless you can *communicate* it to others. This could be in several forms:
   — written — in sentences and paragraphs, or in chart form
   — oral — telling other people
   — graphic — creating *pictures* to illustrate a topic to others

   For this activity, record your information in chart form.

Problem	Description
Financial	
Language	
Etc.	

Optional Activity — A Comparison Chart Then and Now

Problem	Immigration 1815-1850	Immigration Today

By adding an additional column, you could *compare* problems faced by immigrants in the 1815-1860 period with problems faced today.

12. Writing a Research Report or Essay

Two Forms of Reports

1. *Descriptive* Report
   Some historical reports simply describe events:
   The life style of the Inuit before contact with Europeans
   Spiritual beliefs of the Native Peoples
   The achievements of the Mayans and the Aztecs
   The voyages of Jacques Cartier
   Samuel de Champlain, Father of New France
   These reports merely *describe* in a narrative form what happened.

2. *Explanatory* (or expository) Essay
   Writing an explanatory (or expository) essay is more complex and difficult. It involves *more varied research, selection* of material, and *organization.*
   You use this form when you are trying *to explain* an *issue*, or consider a viewpoint (or even an hypothesis) rather than just describe what happened. While your research is being completed, you must form an *opinion, take a point of view,* and try to *prove* your position.

Organization before writing

1. *Research* to collect data on your topic
2. Select one or two questions to *focus* your research on the topic.
3. *Organize* your supporting information or evidence in an appropriate order or sequence
4. Think of an appropriate *conclusion* or consequence to explain why your topic is important or significant.
5. *Record* your introduction, supporting information, and conclusion in a *rough outline.*
6. Your outline should be in point form, and should not be more than one page long.

Your Task

Write a five-paragraph report on one of the following topics:

The reasons for the fall of New France
The deportation of the Acadians
The causes of the American Revolution
The impact of the Loyalists in Canada
Louis Riel — innocent or guilty?

Individualization of Your Program

As teachers, we are aware of the great differences between our students — differences in reading level, differences in ability and interest, differences in aptitude, and differences in learning style. In spite of these differences, in many classes most students are given the same assignments most of the time. This creates frustration for some students, and boredom for others. It is therefore essential that for part of your classroom activities, students have opportunities for choice.

The *Be Creative* section of the pedagogy part of each topic provides opportunities for individualization and creativity.

(1) Students should have some choice of the topic. Students can choose within a range of topics provided, or choose a topic of their own choice.

(2) Students should have some choice of the medium of communication. Students should be able to negotiate or contract with the teacher whether their presentation is a written report, an oral presentation, an interview, a pictorial presentation, a computer print-out, a video, a filmstrip, or a model or diorama.

Teachers should monitor students' choice over the year, but it is essential that students have an opportunity to choose a topic and presentation reflecting their interests. It is often surprising how much extra effort students will put into a task when they have been given the opportunity and responsibility of choice.

For your convenience, the pedagogical activities from the textbook *Origins — A History of Canada*, are provided in the following section by chapter.

The following maps may be reproduced by teachers for student use (non-commercial) in their learning activities.

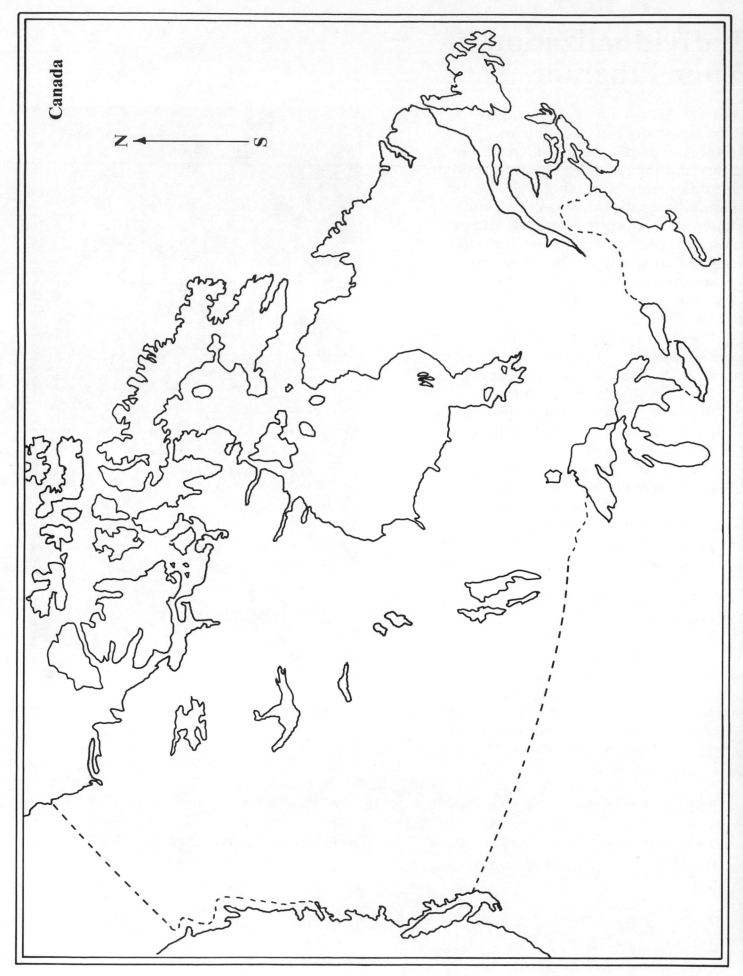

Canada

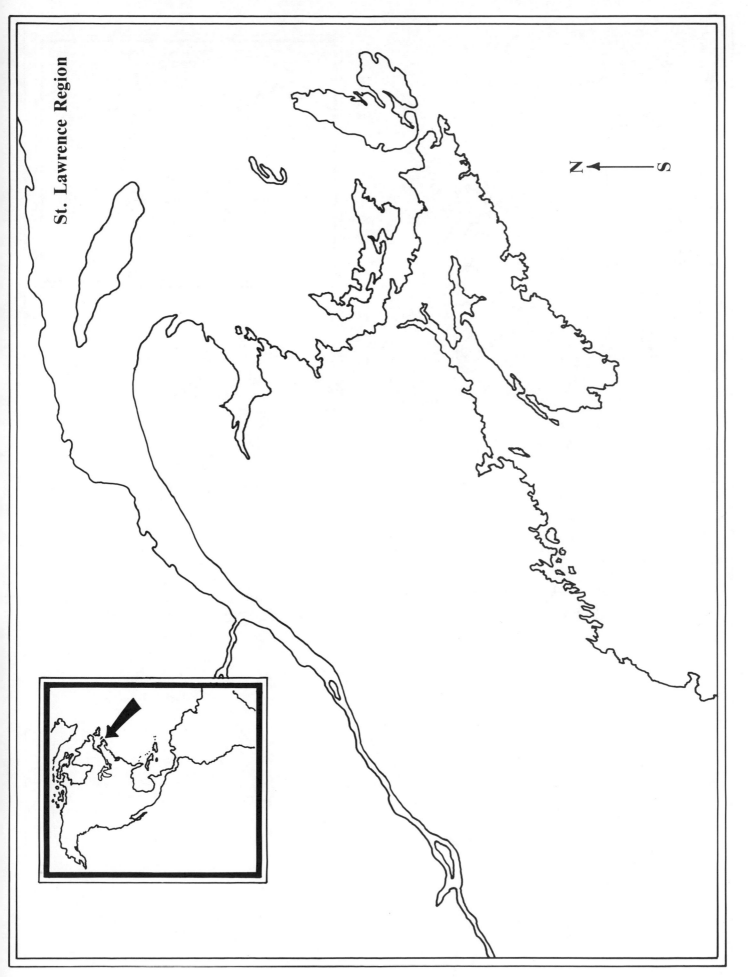

St. Lawrence Region

N ← → S

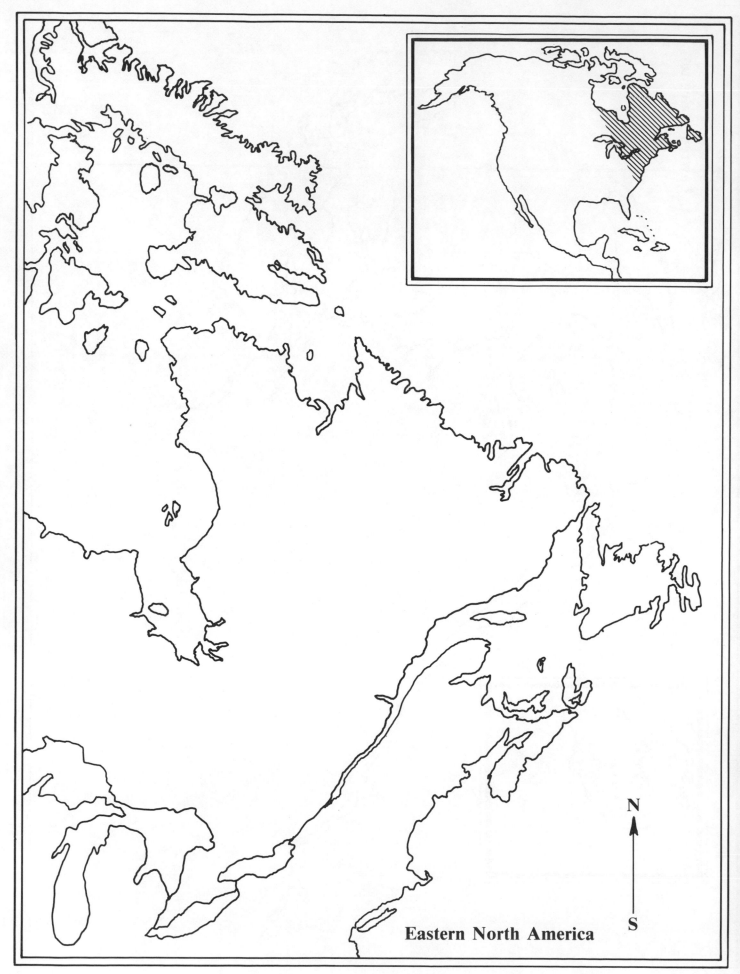

Eastern North America

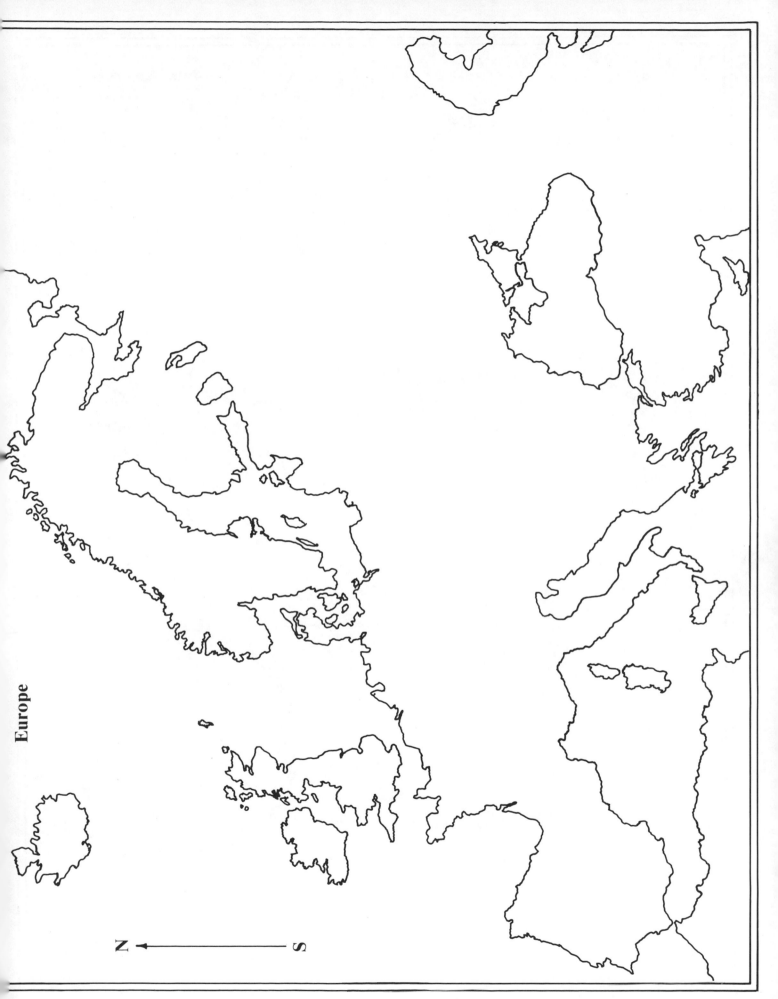

Europe

N ← → S

South America

N
S

CHAPTER ONE / A NEW WORLD

Units 1. The Beginnings
2. Beringia: The Land Bridge
3. Migration through North America
4. The Origins of Humans
5. The Native Peoples

1. The Beginnings (pages 6-9)

Can You Recall?

1. Define the word "pre-historic". Why do we use it to describe that period?
2. Locate the Old Crow River area in the Yukon. Why does much of the evidence used by archaeologists come from this region?

Ideas For Discussion

1. Western scientists and many Native Peoples disagree about when the Indians first came to North America. Why is there a difference of opinion? Which point of view do you support? Explain.
2. Discuss several ways animal bones could have been used by the first Americans.

Research

1. A bone artifact, a flesher, was discovered near the Old Crow River. Different dating techniques have yielded varying results as to the age of this artifact. Write a brief report to explain:
   a) the use of the flesher (a diagram could be drawn)
   b) other artifacts archaeologists have used to determine when the Indians arrived;
   c) your opinion about the accuracy of these methods.

Be Creative

1. Research one of the Indian Creation myths. Present your findings to the class either as a story or as a skit.
2. Imagine you are hunting a giant mammoth. Write a story about the hardships you encounter. Describe: climate; terrain; size and strength of the beast; your need for food; and other concerns you believe need to be mentioned. You may start with: "I have been stalking this mammoth for several days."
3. "Just how long have the Indians been here?"
   Write a brief newspaper report to answer this question. Include some of the following terms: archaeologist, Old Crow River, bones of animals, pre-historic tools, carbon-14, different dating methods.

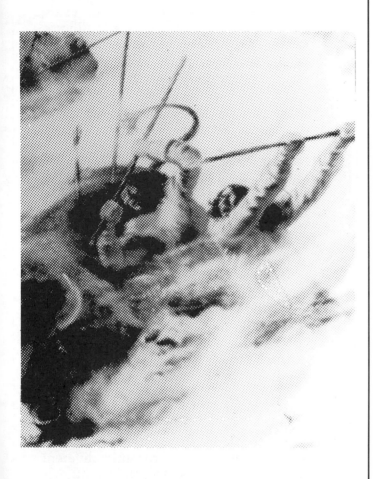

2. Beringia: The Land Bridge (pages 10-13)

Can You Recall?

1. Explain each of the following theories as to how the Native Peoples came to the Americas.
   a) Lost continent theory;
   b) Long ocean journey theory;
   c) Beringia land bridge theory.

Ideas For Discussion

1. Define the term "theory". What makes one theory more acceptable than another?
2. Why is the Beringia Land Bridge Theory accepted more widely than the Lost Continent or Long Ocean Journey Theories? Which theory do you find most believable? Explain.
3. Why is the formation of glaciers considered to be important in the pre-historic history of this continent?

Research

1. Find out more about the theories related to the lost continents of Mu or Atlantis. Present a report outlining:
   a) Who proposed these theories.
   b) What evidence there is to support or to reject these points of view.

Be Creative

1. Draw a poster or write a poem to explain the origins of the Native Peoples and how they got to North America. Give an imaginative title to your poster or poem.
2. Make a series of drawings of the Beringia Land Bridge.
3. Pretend to be a reporter for a large TV network. Your assignment is to present a show to answer the question: "How did the Native Peoples get here and where did they come from?" You must present evidence to answer these questions in an interesting and imaginative way that will improve the network's ratings. Highlight: "on the spot interviews", new evidence, different points of view to attract TV viewers. By the end of the programme, you should present some conclusions to your classroom audience.

3. Migration Through North America (pages 14-17

Do You Recall?

1. Use the following words to retell the story of the arrival of the pre-historic Native Peoples in the Americas. Use each word only once: cultural; thousand; ice-free; nomadic; hunters; South America; Alaska-Yukon; regions; glaciers; 25 000 years; melted; Mackenzie River Valley; Alberta; environments; time; Saskatchewan; space.
2. Give two reasons why anthropologists study pre-historic stone tools, weapons, and arrowheads.
3. What can we learn from the study of different styles of spearpoints?

Ideas For Discussion

1. Over a period of thousands of years, the temperature of the Americas has changed. Tell how these changes would gradually affect the life of the Native Peoples.
   a) the temperature gradually decreases;
   b) the temperature gradually increases;
   c) the water drains away leaving a flat area (i.e., the prairies, the St. Lawrence Lowlands).
2. How would the environment and climate influence the evolution of different native cultural groups throughout North and South America?

Research

1. Research what pre-historic hunting might have involved in terms of: animals hunted; where they were found; different types of spearpoints used; and techniques used to stalk these beasts. How does all of this compare to modern-day hunting?
2. Research more information about glaciers. Your research might indicate *where* and *when* glaciers covered large parts of North America; *why* the glaciers changed size; and the effects of glaciation on such areas as the prairies, the Canadian Shield, or the St. Lawrence Lowlands.

Be Creative

1. Choose one of the following:
   a) Make a drawing of a native hunting a pre-historic animal; or
   b) Write an imaginary report of a hunter pursuing an animal; or
   c) "You are There". Prepare and present an interview with one or two hunters to explain how they hunt.

4. The Origins of Humans (pages 18-21)

Can You Recall?

1. What is the story of creation as described in the Bible?
2. a) Define the term "evolution".
   b) How did Charles Darwin support the theory of evolution in his book *The Origin of Species*?
3. How do many people attempt to balance their religious beliefs and the theory of evolution?
4. Where do scientists generally believe human beings originated? What contributions did Louis and Mary Leakey make to this theory?

Ideas For Discussion

1. After consulting with your parents, teachers, or religious advisors, what do *you* think about the origin of humans?

Research

1. Do a research report on either Charles Darwin, Louis and Mary Leakey, or Donald Johanson. Your report should include:
   b) their area of research or studies;
   c) the nature of their discoveries and theories;
   d) reasons why some people agree or disagree with them;
   e) the importance of their theories on modern views of the origins of humans.
2. Research how anthropologists, archaeologists, and palaeontologists have contributed to our understandings of the origins of humans.

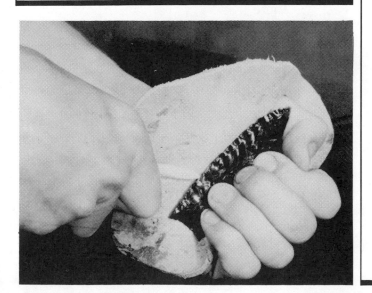

5. The Native Peoples (pages 22-25)

Can You Recall?

1. In what ways are the Bushmen of the Kalahari today similar to the earliest inhabitants of North America?
2. What materials did the earliest inhabitants of North America use to make utensils, tools, and weapons? Why do we usually find artifacts made only of stone?
3. Construct a chart for each of the three major racial groups. For each group, indicate skin colour, colour and form of hair, shape of head, stature, form of nose, and eye colour.

Ideas For Discussion

1. In what ways is looking at the pre-historic past like looking at the distant future?

Research

1. "We can get an idea of the life led by the first North Americans from modern Bushmen who are some of the very few people on earth today who still carry on a way of life that has hardly changed at all since humans first evolved."

   Keep the above statement in mind while you research the Bushmen to learn more about their physical appearance, society, and way of life.
2. Choose two different Native groups from different parts of North or South America. Research the differences and similarities of these two groups, as well as how the environment influences their lifestyle.

Be Creative

1. After researching further information on the pre-historic Native Peoples, do one of the following:
   a) write an imaginary "day-in-the-life-of" a native person;
   b) do a series of drawings to illustrate the "everyday" life of a North American Stone Age Indian;
   c) write a poem or short story on how the Native Peoples gradually adapted to different environments;
   d) build a Paleo-Indian model village using clay, tooth picks, and popsicle sticks. Show how the environment affected the construction of their shelters. Include labels and a brief written explanation of your model.

Units 1. The Environment
2. The Inuit
3. Before European Contact
4. Spiritual Beliefs
5. Native Communications

1. The Environment (pages 26-31)

Can You Recall?

Complete the following chart in your workbook.

REGION	CLIMATE	VEGETATION	PHYSICAL FEATURES
The Arctic			
The SubArctic			
The Eastern Woodlands and Great Lakes			
The Great Plains			
The West Coast			
The Western High Plateau			

Ideas For Discussion

1. In which region would you choose to live? Why?
2. In which region would you dislike living? Why?

Research

1. a) Identify an industry or occupation that presently exists in your area and explain why it is suitable for your environment.

   b) Find out about an industry that is located in one other region, and explain why it is suitable to be located there.

2. Find out which native groups still live in a traditional region. How have their lives been influenced by the physical environment of the area?

Be Creative

1. Divide the class into six groups. Each group should create a section for a mural of all the regions of Canada.
2. Write a diary pretending to be one of the first settlers in one of the regions.
3. Role-play a meeting of Native Peoples from two very different regions.

2. The Inuit (pages 32-35)

Can You Recall?
1. Match the title with the correct description.
   a) The First Inuit: Thule People
   b) People of the Arctic: Small Tool Tradition
   c) "Old Eskimos" or Paleo-Eskimos
   d) Bering Strait Land Bridge
   e) The Dorset Culture
      i) lived in small nomadic bands of one or two families
      ii) used as a route to the northwestern tip of North America
      iii) considered to be the original occupants of the Arctic
      iv) developed in the region of Northern Hudson Bay, Hudson Strait, and Foxe Basin
      v) considered to be the earliest Inuit people most likely to meet Europeans

Ideas For Discussion
1. Why is the Bering Strait Land Bridge a key factor in explaining the arrival of the Inuit in North America?
2. Why do Canadian Eskimos want to be know as "Inuit" instead of "Eskimos"?
3. What aspects of Thule culture allowed them to become more advanced than the Paleo-Eskimos and Dorset People?
4. Why was the Inuit way of life one of the last to be affected by the arrival of Europeans in Canada?

Research
1. Prepare a report on one of the following:
   a) Paleo-Eskimos; b) Dorset People;
   c) Thule Culture.
   In your report use the following headings:
   Location; Food; Clothing; Shelter; Tools and Weapons; Transportation;
   Social Structure.
   Include drawings, graphs, and a map, as well as descriptive notes.

Be Creative
1. Make a display and a poster showing the way of life of one of the early Inuit groups you have studied. Include the following topics: food; clothing; shelter; tools; transportation; location.

3. Before European Contact (pages 36-39)

Can You Recall?
1. The natives made use of the trees and animals of their environment. Explain the various uses of the following:
   a) deer in the Eastern Woodland;
   b) birch trees in the Eastern Woodland;
   c) seals in the Arctic;
   d) buffalo on the prairies.

Ideas for Discussion
1. The Natives of the Northwest Coast are often called "people of the sea". Discuss the importance of the sea to these people.
2. Describe the environment of the: Eastern Woodlands Region; Northwest Coast Region; Arctic Region; and the Prairie Region. Discuss the ways in which each of these environments affected the lifestyles of the people who lived there.

Research
1. The buffalo was like a "supermarket on hooves" to the people of the plains. Research the various ways in which they used the buffalo.
2. Totem poles made up an important part of the Northwest Coast Native's lifestyle. Prepare a report on totem poles. Include various examples of symbols or designs.
3. Make a report describing the way of life of one of the Eastern Woodlands nations. Use the following headings: Hunting; Shelter; Clothing; Games, Dances, and Celebrations; The Spirit World.
4. Prepare a report that describes how the Inuit survived in such a harsh environment.

Be Creative
1. Make a model or draw pictures comparing the various types of shelter used by Native Peoples in the different regions across Canada.
2. Construct a model of a totem pole that might have been used by one of the Northwest Coast nations.
3. Write a poem that describes the way of life of one of the Native groups that you have studied.

4. Spiritual Beliefs (pages 40-43)

Can You Recall?

1. The Native Peoples believed that all living things have a "soul". How did this affect their beliefs about their relationship with the plants and animals of their environment?

2. Why is the Native Peoples' belief that everything is interrelated basic to their view of nature?

3. What is the difference between the Biblical view of nature and the native idea of a "web" of life?

Ideas For Discussion

1. What can we learn from the natives' respect for nature? How can it help ensure the well-being of our environment?

2. "Historically Indians have tried to live in a 'symbiotic' relationship with nature, not tried to dominate." (symbiotic — living together in a co-operative relationship)
   a) Give at least one example of how we live in a co-operative relationship with nature today.
   b) Give at least one example of our exploitive (non-symbiotic) relationship with nature today.
   c) What are the likely consequences of each of these attitudes?
   d) How do the attitudes towards hunting differ between Native Peoples and other hunters?

Research

1. Learn more about the environmental problems or concerns in your community. How might the Native Peoples' attitude towards nature help deal with these issues?

2. Prepare a report that focuses on recent native land claims and environmental concerns in at least two areas of Canada.

Be Creative

1. Draw an environmental poster that illustrates the Native Peoples' concerns and respect for nature.

2. Write a poem or prepare a skit that contrasts the Native Peoples' view of nature with that of our industrial society.

3. Debate: Resolved that the native view of nature as a "web of life" is preferable to the Christian idea of nature as a pyramid.

5. Native Communications (pages 44-45)

Can You Recall?

1. Why is it difficult to study the "Indian language"?

2. How many Indian languages and language families are there in Canada?

3. Locate where each of the following language groups were found: Inuktitut; Athabaskan; Algonquian; Siouan; Iroquoian; Kutenai and Salish.

Ideas For Discussion

1. Why was it necessary for the Native Peoples to develop a sign language?

Research

1. Prepare a report on:
   a) sign language used by deaf people;
   b) Morse Code;
   c) Flag signals.

2. Find out how and why Canadian Indians are attempting to preserve and promote their native languages.

3. a) What are the native languages and language families found within Canada today?
   b) Find a map that illustrates the above information.

Be Creative

1. a) Play a game of Charades, using only terms related to Native Peoples.
   b) What problems of communication are revealed by Charades? How does the use of language solve many of these problems? What problems exist even when we speak the same language?

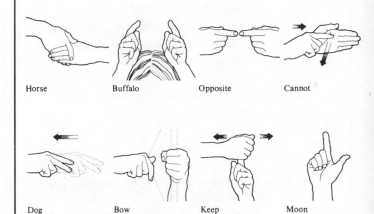

Horse   Buffalo   Opposite   Cannot

Dog   Bow   Keep   Moon

CHAPTER THREE / LOST CIVILIZATIONS

Units 1. Native Government
      2. Farming
      3. Mayas and Aztecs
      4. Trade
      5. Disease

1. Native Government (pages 46-49)

Can You Recall?

1. What is meant by "a confederation"?
2. What is meant by
   — The Canadian Confederation?
   — The Iroquois Confederation?
3. Why did several tribes create confederations in the 1400s?
4. Draw a map showing:
   a) The six nations of the Iroquois Confederacy;
   b) The Huron Confederacy.

Ideas For Discussion

1. Why is it necessary to have a government in any society?
2. "Both the Huron Confederacy and the Iroquois League functioned as participatory democracies." What is a "participatory" democracy? How is that different from a "representative democracy"? What are the advantages and disadvantages of such a system of government?

Research

1. Do research on the Iroquois League or the Huron Confederacy in terms of:
   a) why they were formed;
   b) who belonged to them;
   c) how they were democratically organized.
2. Find out more about women's roles in Huron and Iroquoian government. How does it compare with modern Canadian women's political roles?
3. How is your local government organized? Is it similar to how the Huron and Iroquois Confederacies were set up? Explain.

Be Creative

1. Draw a flag or crest that would represent the different aspects of either the Huron or the Iroquois confederations.
2. Review what a Huron Confederation meeting would have probably been like. Select a concern that they might have dealt with at the time (e.g., raids from a neighbouring tribe or the arrival of European fur traders). Re-enact a gathering of the representatives from the different tribes and villages as they attempt to deal with the issue at hand.

2. Farming (pages 50-53)

Can You Recall?

1. What were the first plants grown in the Americas?
2. What is meant by "agricultural revolution"? What were at least four changes brought by the change from "hunting and gathering" to "agriculture"?
3. Explain how and when agriculture spread from Central America to the area inhabited by the Iroquoians.

Ideas For Discussion

1. Debate: Resolved that the ability to grow food is the main factor in the growth of a society.
2. How would the lifestyles of early native hunters and gatherers be different from that of farmers? (Consider size of population, homes, food, life expectancy, arts and crafts, system of government.)

Research

1. Research the nature of agriculture carried out by the Olmecs or Mayas in Mexico.
2. Research how agriculture was carried on by the Iroquois. Your report should include crops grown, methods of agriculture, roles of females, males, and children, and the influences on their society.
3. Some farmers in Canada and other parts of the world are experiencing great difficulties today.
   a) Find out some of the problems faced by farmers in your own area, or in other parts of Canada.
   b) If many farmers in Canada went bankrupt or ceased producing food, what problems would be created for you and other Canadians?
4. Prepare a report that examines areas of the world that suffer from food shortages today (e.g., northeast Africa, southeast Asia). Find out what geographical or political factors affect these areas and cause the food shortages.

Be Creative

1. Prepare a picture, with explanations to show:
   a) native agriculture in ancient Mexico;
   b) agriculture in an Iroquoian village.
2. Prepare a collage of newspaper headlines that deal with agricultural and food production issues from around the world.

3. Mayas and Aztecs (pages 54-59)

Can You Recall?

1. Locate the Maya, Aztec, and Inca Empires on a map of Meso-America and South America.
2. How did agriculture contribute to the development of these civilizations?
3. Describe the chief characteristics and achievements and the time period of the following civilizations: Olmec; Maya; Aztec, Inca.
4. Locate on a map, and describe the importance of: Teotihuacan (Maya); Machu Picchu (Inca)

Research

1. Do some research on one of the classical civilizations of Meso-America. Your report should include some of the following: their system of agriculture; homes; architecture and buildings; artifacts and crafts; religious beliefs.
2. Prepare a report on the ancient city of Teotihuacan or Machu Picchu.
3. "The Mayas and Aztecs and the Incas have often been described as the Greeks and Romans of the Americas."
   Research some information about Greece and Rome to explain why this is an accurate statement.

Be Creative

1. Make a display or poster of the life of one of the Central or South American native groups. Include: food, clothing, shelter, transportation, art, religion, as well as contributions to our modern way of life.
2. Obtain brochures about Mexico, and the different Central and South American countries from a travel agent. Prepare a pictorial display that highlights tourist attractions that focus on the history and development of one of these countries.
3. Prepare a news report for your class focusing on the achievements of the ancient civilizations of Central and South America.
4. Prepare a collage of newspaper headlines that deal with some of the issues and concerns of modern Mexico, Central and South America.

4. Trade (pages 60-63)

Can You Recall?

1. Trace the water routes by which goods were traded between the southern part of the continent to the Great Lakes region.
2. What were three of the main trade items in pre-European Canada, and what were their uses?
3. Explain how the Natives of Mexico eventually influenced the food of the Iroquois natives.

Ideas For Discussion

1. What advantages and disadvantages would there be for different native groups in trading with each other during pre-European times?
2. Discuss how trade with another country (e.g., Japan) affects our lifestyle today.

Research

1. Find out which foods and products, that we use today, were originally developed by the ancient civilizations of Meso- and South America.
2. Find out more about the "pueblo" civilization and how its influence is still seen in modern New Mexico and Arizona.
3. What is the Serpent Mound at Rice Lake, southeast of Peterborough? Why is it considered important to a study of the mound builder culture?

Be Creative

1. Trace or sketch an outline of North America. Highlight the major water networks that were and are still used for transporting and trading goods.
2. Write a short story. Pretend to be an archaeologist working at a site near Rice Lake. Imagine that you have discovered the graves of numerous individuals who lived thousands of years ago. Tell how you felt and what you learned as you dug deeper into the past.
3. Design a poster that illustrates the importance of trade in the development of a society.

5. Disease (pages 64-67)

Can You Recall?

1. Explain why, after the arrival of the Europeans, the Indian population was reduced by as much as 90%.
2. Approximately how many Native Peoples lived in Canada, the United States, Mexico, and Central and South America by the time the first Europeans began to arrive in the early 1500s?
3. Approximately how many registered Indians and Inuit live in Canada today? How many more have some degree of native ancestry?
4. According to some theories, why were there no widespread epidemics on the North American continent before the Europeans' arrival?

Ideas For Discussion

1. How might the history of the North and South American continents have been different if the Native Peoples had not been so adversely affected by the deadly diseases brought from Europe?
2. Are there any examples in the world today of diseases being transmitted between peoples of different countries or continents? How might these problems be reduced?

Research

1. Prepare a report on the disease "smallpox". What is it? What causes it? What is being done to prevent its spread?
2. How has medical science helped to rid society of the spread of such diseases as influenza, typhus, and cholera?
3. Are there any groups of people today who have been plagued by the spread of deadly diseases? Why has this happened? What is being done to prevent or control it?

Be Creative

1. Write a prayer by a native person explaining his or her attitude about the arrival of Europeans and their deadly diseases.
2. Role-play a situation in the 1600s where an American Native and a European have met. The topic of the conversation should focus on how the Native feels about what is happening as a result of the spread of new diseases.

CHAPTER FOUR / THE FIRST EUROPEANS

Units 1. The Viking Explorations
2. First Viking Settlements
3. The Brendan Voyage
4. Exploration by Sea
5. Italian Merchant Traders

1. The Viking Explorations (pages 68-71)

Can You Recall

1. Who were the Norsemen and where did they live? Why did they set out on voyages that eventually led them to North America? What were the Icelandic sagas?
2. Describe the voyages and importance of a) Eric the Red; b) Leif Ericsson.
3. Give the probable locations of: Helluland; Markland; Vinland.
4. L'Anse-aux-Meadows: Describe this first European settlement in North America (location, when discovered, date of settlement, buildings).

Ideas For Discussion

1. It is commonly stated that Columbus "discovered" America. Discuss this statement from the viewpoint of:
   a) a Viking explorer; b) a native person.
2. Why have the Viking voyagers not had the recognition that other European explorers have had?

Research

1. Research further information on the Viking explorations of the Americas.
2. Research further information on the nature of Viking life in Scandinavia.
3. Read further on the Icelandic sagas. Select an interesting story and read it to your fellow students.
4. Do a report on L'Anse-aux-Meadows. Describe what we know about the settlement, the people, the buildings, the relationships with the Natives, and the end of the settlement.

Be Creative

1. The Vikings were excellent shipbuilders. Find out more about their ships. Make a drawing of one of their ships. Present this, with explanation, to your classmates.
2. Write an imaginative description, in the style of the Icelandic sagas, of one of the Viking voyages to the Americas.

2. First Viking Settlements (pages 72-75)

Can You Recall?

1. Locate the first settlement at L'Anse-aux-Meadows.
2. Describe the original meeting between the Vikings led by Karlsefni and "skraelings" (natives).
3. What factors led to the failure of the Viking settlement at L'Anse-aux-Meadows?

Ideas For Discussion

1. The first explorers claimed that the land they "discovered" "belonged" to them.
   a) To what degree can you say that Europeans discovered the New World?
   b) Who had the right to the lands which the Vikings claimed — the natives or the Viking settlers?
2. "The ancient Vikings were not so different from the thousands of immigrants who have come to this country with the very same dreams." To what degree is this true? In what ways are modern immigrants *similar* to the Viking settlers? In what ways are modern immigrants *different* from the Viking settlers?

Research

1. What is meant by the term "aboriginal rights"? To what degree do the Native Peoples of Canada still claim aboriginal rights in Canada?
2. Do research on the nature of the colony at L'Anse-aux-Meadows. Prepare a diagram with explanations of the main buildings and activities which have recently been discovered.

Be Creative

1. Make a drawing of a Viking long boat (*draker*). Label the different parts. Explain how the boat was propelled by sail and by oars.
2. Role-play or prepare a skit on the first meeting of the Vikings and the Native Peoples.
3. Write an imaginary description of life at L'Anse-aux-Meadows, giving the reasons why the colony was finally abandoned.

3. The Brendan Voyage (pages 76-77)

For Recall and Discussion

1. Describe the voyage of Timothy Severin in the 1970s, from Ireland to Newfoundland. What did he try to prove by this voyage?
2. Describe what we know about the original Brendan voyage of around 560 A.D. Do you believe that this voyage actually happened? Explain your answer.
3. Describe the probable construction of St. Brendan's boat.

Research

1. Do further research on:
   a) St. Brendan;
   b) Timothy Severin's voyage.

CHAPTER FOUR / THE FIRST EUROPEANS

4. Exploration by Sea (pages 78-81)

Can You Recall?

1. Explain the meaning of the following terms:
   Orient; Pilgrimage; Islam; Muslim; Pilgrim.
2. Why were there attempts by the Christians to "liberate" the Christian holy places in the Middle East?
3. Explain what is meant by the term "Crusades"? Describe the key events of one of the Crusades.
4. In the 1400s, the Turkish empire gained control of these trade routes to the Orient. How did this lead to a burst of European exploration towards the end of the 15th century?

Ideas For Discussion

1. Do further research on one of the Crusades. To what degree were the crusaders motivated by religion; seeking riches; sense of adventure; other reasons?
2. Do you believe that Europeans had the right to fight to liberate the Holy Land? Discuss this from the viewpoint of: a European Christian; a Turkish Muslim.

Research

1. Do research on the key beliefs of Islam. Explain the importance of: Mohamed; the Koran; some of the important religious beliefs; the extent of Islam in the world today.
2. Do research on one of the Crusades. In your report, explain the following aspects of the Crusades: the leader(s); where the Crusaders came from; their motives or reasons for joining the Crusade; their route of travel; why it was important.
3. The contact with the Muslims resulted in awareness of new products and new ideas. Find out the Muslim contributions to the Western World as far as products; and influences on medicine, mathematics, and chemistry.

Be Creative

1. Write a letter of: a) a knight describing his experiences on a Crusade; b) a Crusader's lady about her life at home; c) a Muslim who resisted the Crusaders.

5. Italian Merchant Traders (pages 82-87)

Can You Recall?

1. How did the Portuguese explorers Bartholomeu Dias and Vasco da Gama attempt to reach the riches of the Orient?
2. Describe the route of the first (1492) and second (1493) and third (1498) voyages of Christopher Columbus. Why is he important? What error did he make?
3. Why did Cabot want to seek a northwest passage to the Orient? Describe the route of Cabot's voyage in 1497. What was the importance of his voyage?

Ideas For Discussion

1. Columbus is famous as the person who discovered America. Why is his voyage considered to be more important than those of Brendan, the Vikings, or other explorers?

Research

1. Do a project about Columbus or Cabot. Include: the background of the explorer; why he sailed; who financed the voyage; route of exploration (map); fears or anxieties of the explorer; kind of ship or technology used for the voyage; what was accomplished.
2. Make a labelled drawing of a ship seen by either Columbus or Cabot. Explain the difficulties of sailing across the Atlantic on such a ship.

Be Creative

1. The exploration of the world did not end in the 15th century. In fact, it is still continuing. Select a field of modern exploration (e.g., Space, Oceanic Surveys, the Antarctic, Mountain Climbing, or Scientific Research).

   Using headings similar to those in the research activity for Columbus or Cabot, research one area of modern exploration: why the exploration is being carried out; fears or anxieties of participant; financial support; technology used; accomplishment. Present your reports to other members of the class.
2. "You are There" — After researching Columbus or Cabot, write and act an imaginary T.V. interview with the explorer.

CHAPTER FIVE / THE TREASURE HUNT

Units 1. The Pope Divides the World
2. Decline of English and Portuguese Interest in Newfoundland
3. Fishing
4. Age of Exploration
5. The Europeans Meet the Native Peoples

1. The Pope Divides the New World (pages 88-91)

Can You Recall?

1. Why did Columbus' discovery of gold in the Americas lead to a danger of war?
2. a) In the Treaty of Tordesillas of 1497 (the Pope's Line), how were the Americas divided? What were the permanent results in South America?
   b) Draw the line on a map of the Americas. Who benefitted most — Spain or Portugal?
   c) Why did Portugal turn its interest to the north — to Newfoundland?

Ideas for Discussion

1. Why does the discovery of gold always arouse great interest?
2. How might the Americas be different today if the Pope's Line had been drawn farther to the west?

Research

1. Do a report on the Papacy. In your report, explain such things as the role of the Pope; the Vatican; the influence of the papacy among Roman Catholics.
2. Pope Alexander VI was responsible for the Treaty of Tordesillas, 1497. Research his family background, and some of his ideas. Why would he be considered one of the least successful Popes?

2. Decline of English and Portuguese Interest In Newfoundland (pages 92-95)

3. Fishing (pages 96-99)

Can You Recall?

1. Write a three-paragraph report on the voyages of John Cabot. Write one paragraph to describe each of the following topics:
   a) the voyage of 1497, and reasons for Henry VII's disappointment;
   b) reasons why the King agreed to finance a second voyage in 1498;
   c) 1498 — second voyage — what happened and the results for Henry VII.

2. Write a brief note on the voyages of each of the following Portuguese. In each voyage, explain when, why, where, what they did, and the importance of
   - Fernandez de Lavrador;
   - Corté Réal;
   - Fagundes.

3. Draw a map of the area of Newfoundland and the east coast of North America showing the routes of the voyages of
   - Cabot;
   - de Lavrador;
   - Corté Réal;
   - Fagundes.

Be Creative

1. Research the explorations of *one* of the above explorers.

2. Prepare a presentation for the rest of the class in one of the following ways:
   a) a TV interview with the explorer;
   b) a research report;
   c) an imaginary letter written by the explorer describing his voyages, his feelings, his impressions;
   d) a series of drawings representing aspects of the voyage of exploration (i.e., ships, sailors, meeting with natives);
   e) a skit representing a meeting of the explorer with local natives;
   f) a skit representing conversations of Henry VII and Cabot, between 1497 and 1498.

Can You Recall?

1. Prepare a report on fishing off the Grand Banks, organizing your answers around the following headings:
   a) Why fish are so abundant in this area;
   b) Why fish were an important source of food in the 16th century;
   c) The different nations that fished in this area in the 14th to 16th centuries.

2. Describe the process of drying fish. Why was this an essential process for people in the 16th century?

Research

1. Prepare a report on the reasons for the importance of fish in medieval Europe.

2. Today, we are increasing the amount of fish eaten by each person. Prepare a report on the nutritional values of fish in medieval times and in our diets today.

4. Age of Exploration (pages 100-103)

Can You Recall?

1. Make a record of the following explorers, in either chart or paragraph form. a) Amerigo Vespucci; b) Ferdinand Magellan; c) Giovanni da Verrazano.

    Make sure that your report includes the following organizers: Country of Origin; Date of Voyage; Reason for Exploration; Accomplishments; Importance of Significance; Map showing voyage(s).

2. What was the most important contribution of
    a) Vespucci?
    b) Magellan?
    c) Verrazano?

Be Creative

1. Have a panel discussion for the class. One student will represent Columbus, Vespucci, Magellan, and Verrazano. Each person will describe his voyages and try to prove *who* was the greatest explorer. The class can ask questions of each explorer. At the end, the class will vote as to who was the greatest explorer.

2. Draw a picture of a ship used by one of the early explorers and label the parts.

3. Write an imaginary letter from one of the explorers, describing the voyage and explaining its importance.

4. Divide the class into groups of four students. Each group is to prepare a folder on one explorer. The folder should include a map showing the voyage route; a drawing of a ship of the period; a description of the voyage; a series of diary entries about the voyage; a cover for the folder, illustrating the voyage in a graphic way. Groups should present their information to the class in as interesting a manner as possible (e.g., T.V. interviews, panel reports, use of overhead transparencies, display of pictures or graphics, skit presentations, etc.).

5. The Europeans Meet the Native Peoples (pages 104-109)

Can You Recall?

1. Write two reports in paragraph or chart form about:
    a) the conquest of the Aztecs by Cortés;
    b) the conquest of the Incas by Pizarro.
    The organizers should be:
    Name of conquistador; Country of origin; Date of conquest; Map showing route of conquest; Attitude of the conquistadores; Attitude of the natives; Technological advantages of the Spanish; Results of conquest.

Ideas For Discussion

1. The Spanish conquistadores assumed that they had the right of conquest because of their superiority. Why did they feel superior? Was that attitude justified then? Would it be justified today?

2. Can you think of any examples in the world today where a country is "successful" in conquering a weaker people, where some people might question the morality (rightness or wrongness) of this conquest.

For Research

1. Tenochtitlan was one of the largest cities in the world in 1500. Prepare a report on at least one of the following for your class:
    a) buildings and temples;
    b) religion of the people.

2. Montezuma was one of the world's great leaders. Do some research on his accomplishments. Report to the class by:
    a) an interview with Montezuma;
    b) a written report on his deeds.

3. Do a class report on the artistic achievements of the Mayas or Aztecs (e.g., jewellery, pottery, other arts and crafts).

4. The Incas were famous for building roads, bridges, terraces, canals, and aqueducts. Describe how at least three of these were built, and why they were important.

5. Write a report on the religious beliefs of the Aztecs or Incas. Include such organizers as religious beliefs, temples, role of priests, role of human sacrifice.

Be Creative

1. Hold a court of law in which either Cortés or Pizarro is on trial for murder. Class members should research the case and play the judge, prosecuting lawyer, defence lawyer, witnesses, jurors, clerks of the court. All other members of the class act as reporters to write up the trial.

CHAPTER SIX / THE KEY TO CANADA

Units 1. Cartier Discovers the St. Lawrence
2. Cartier's Contacts with the Native Peoples
3. Cartier's First Canadian Winter
4. Cartier's Third Voyage, 1541
5. Fool's Gold

1. Cartier Discovers the St. Lawrence (pages 110-113)

Can You Recall?

1. On a map, locate and label Cartier's routes.
— 1534 - Voyage #1 — locate and label Newfoundland, Prince Edward Island, Gaspé Peninsula, Anticosti Island, Strait of Belle Isle, "The Land God Gave to Cain".
— 1535-6 - Voyage #2 — St. Lawrence River, Stadacona (Quebec), Hochelaga (Montreal)

Ideas For Discussion

1. Explain the meaning of the following;
the "land God gave to Cain";
the "Bay of Chaleur";
The St. Lawrence — "the key to Canada."

Research

1. Draw and label a picture of one of Cartier's ships.
2. After researching Cartier's voyages,
— conduct an interview with Jacques Cartier, asking him to describe his first impressions of his voyage to North America; *or*
— write a diary by Cartier describing his experiences on the voyages; *or*
— write a newspaper account of Cartier's explorations.

2. Cartier's Contacts With the Native Peoples (pages 114-119)

3. Cartier's First Canadian Winter (pages 120-121)

Can You Recall?

1. Identify these places — Stadacona, Hochelaga, Mount Royal, Kanata.
2. How did the Native Peoples treat Cartier and the French from 1534 to 1536?
3. Cartier erected a cross at Gaspé on July 24, 1534.
   a) What did Cartier mean by erecting this cross?
   b) How did the natives react to this cross?

Ideas For Discussion

1. Cartier and the French claimed all of the land of "Kanata" for France. On what basis did they believe they had the right to claim all of this land? How would the natives see this differently? With whom do you agree?
2. Class debate: Resolved that Cartier and the French had the right to claim the lands of the St. Lawrence for France.

Be Creative

YOU ARE THERE

1. After further research on Cartier's voyages, do a TV interview with Cartier to explore his viewpoints as to why he explored the Americas, the difficulties of his voyages, what he observed, his viewpoint of the Natives, the significance of erecting the cross at Gaspé in 1534.
2. After further research, do a TV interview with a native chieftain (e.g., Donnacona) to show his viewpoint of the arrival of the Europeans, how they were treated, his reactions to the cross at Gaspé, and his reactions on being "kidnapped" and taken to France.

Can You Recall?

1. Describe the problems faced by the French settlers
   a) with winter;
   b) with food.
2. What causes scurvy?
   What were the effects on the French?
   How did the natives help the French to survive the winter?
3. How did Cartier treat Donnacona and the other Natives?
4. What were the stories told by the Natives about the "Kingdom of the Saguenay"? Why did these stories excite Cartier?

4. Cartier's Third Voyage (pages 122-125)

Can You Recall?

1. a) Why did the French lose interest in "New France" between 1536 and 1541?

   b) How did the Pope assist in encouraging a renewed interest by the French in New France?

2. a) Who was Jean-François de Roberval?

   b) What was his aim in establishing a permanent colony in New France in the 1540s?

3. a) Locate the route of Cartier's Third Voyage (1541-1542) on a map.

   b) Describe the difficulties of the voyage to the St. Lawrence.

   c) What had happened to Donnacona and the other captives since 1536?

   d) Describe the attempt at a permanent settlement at Cap-Rouge near Stadacona (Quebec)?

4. Why did Roberval's colony fail?

Ideas for Discussion

1. The Iroquois attacked Cartier's settlement in Quebec in 1541. They were often described as "hostile savages" by the Europeans. Is this a fair assessment?

2. How would you account for the hostility of the Iroquois towards French settlers?

Be Creative

1. In summary, the three major problems that French settlers found were:
   a) the Canadian winter;
   b) scurvy and other disease;
   c) relationships with the natives.

   In groups of four or five, prepare a role-play to depict how you would have dealt with these problems more successfully than Cartier and his men.

5. Fool's Gold (pages 126-127)

Can You Recall?

1. Why did Cartier call the rapids on the St. Lawrence River west of Montreal, the "La Chine" Rapids? Why were these rapids an obstacle to exploration?

2. What stories did the natives tell about the Kingdom of the Saguenay? Where was it supposed to be? Why did it continue to arouse interest in French explorers and the French King?

3. a) Why did the discovery of rocks containing iron pyrites and quartz crystals raise the hopes of Cartier?

   b) What is the meaning of the expression "as false as Canadian diamonds"?

Ideas For Discussion

1. Do you believe that the Kingdom of the Saguenay was a myth, or was it based on reality?

Research

1. Research the mineral riches of the Kirkland Lake area, and report to the class.

Be Creative

1. Prepare a role-play of Cartier's presentation of his new minerals to the French king and his experts.

2. Prepare a T.V. interview with Cartier, in the last years of his life, looking back on the successes and disappointments of his career.

Units 1. Effects of Religious Wars on French Exploration
2. Religion in the Americas
3. First English Claim in the Americas
4. A Quest for the Northwest Passage
5. Whaling

1. Effects of Religious Wars on French Exploration (pages 128-129)

Can You Recall?

1. Explain the following terms:

   Roman Catholic Church; Martin Luther; indulgences; Protestants; Huguenots; St. Bartholomew's Day Massacre (1571)

2. Why did the religious wars in France prevent further French exploration in New France in the latter part of the 16th century?

Research

1. Do research on one of the following, and report to the class.
   a) The attitudes of the Roman Catholic Church towards Protestants in the 16th century.
   b) The beliefs of Martin Luther about the Roman Catholic Church.
   c) The beliefs of the Huguenots.

A View of a Stage & also of ye manner of Fishing for, Curing & Drying Cod at NEW FOUND LAND. A. The Habit of ye Fishermen. B. The Line. C. The manner of Fishing. D. The Dressers of ye Fish. E. The Trough into which they throw ye Cod when Dressed. F. Salt Boxes. G. The manner of Carrying ye Cod. H. The Cleansing ye Cod. I. A Press to extract ye Oyl from ye Cods Livers. K. Casks to receive ye Water & Blood that comes from ye Livers. L. Another Cask to receive the Oyl. M. The manner of Drying ye Cod.

2. Religion in the Americas (pages 130-131)

Can You Recall?
1. Explain the terms:
   Catholic Counter-Reformation;
   Jesuit order;
   Spanish missions.
2. By the 1600s, what did the Spanish and Portuguese leaders see as their goal for their American colonies?
   a) resources;
   b) religious goals.
3. Draw a map showing the extent of the Spanish and Portuguese empires by the early 1600s.

Research
The Roman Catholic Church has always played a major role in Latin American countries. Usually, it has been a strong supporter of the policies of the government.

Do further research on one country of Central or South America today. See if you can find an example of how the church today:
a) supports the government in power.
b) opposes some of the ideas of the government in power.

Present your report to the class in the form of a panel discussion or written report.

Topic: The role of the church in Latin America today.

3. First English Claim in the Americas (pages 132-135)

Can You Recall?
1. Explain two reasons for conflict between Spain and England: religious; attacks of the "sea dogs".
2. Describe the objective of the Spanish Armada (1588) and what actually happened.
3. a) Describe the attempts at colonization by Sir Walter Raleigh on Roanoke Island (Virginia) in the 1580s.
   b) Why was the area called "Virginia"?
4. Describe the attempt of Sir Humphrey Gilbert to establish a claim to Newfoundland in 1583.

Ideas For Discussion
1. Drake and the other sea dogs were perceived as heroic daredevils in England, but as ruthless pirates in Spain. With which do you agree?
   a) in a 16th century setting;
   b) in the 20th century.
2. Debate: Resolved that Drake and the other English captains should have been jailed rather than treated as heroes.

Research
1. Do research on one of the following topics, and prepare a brief written report:
   a) The origins of the Church of England;
   b) The Spanish Armada;
   c) The raids of Drake and the Roanoke colony established by Raleigh.
2. a) Make a labelled diagram of: a Spanish galleon (ship); an English ship at the time of the Spanish Armada.
   b) Record the advantages and disadvantages of each.
   c) How do you account for the victory of the English?

Be Creative
Do one of the following: " You Are There".
1. Prepare an interview with either King Philip or Francis Drake to discuss the raids of the sea dogs and the Spanish Armada.
2. Write a newspaper account of the battle of the Spanish Armada.
3. Write an imaginary letter from the viewpoint of either a Spanish sailor or captain, or of Sir francis Drake or an English sailor.
4. Prepare an interview with Elizabeth I to have her explain the greatness of England in her reign.

4. A Quest for the Northwest Passage (pages 136-141)

5. Whaling (pages 142-145)

Can You Recall?

1. Prepare a chart titled "Search for a Northwest Passage" for the following — Gilbert, Drake, Frobisher, Hudson, Amundsen, the *St. Roch*, and the *Manhattan*. Use the following headings (or organizers) for your chart: Date; Exploration route; Achievement.

2. On a map of North America, locate the route of : Davis, Frobisher, Hudson, Amundsen, *St. Roch*, *Manhattan*.

Research

1. Prepare a report or an interview with *one* of the following on their voyage: one of the 16th-century explorers; Roald Amundsen; captain of the *Manhattan*; captain of a modern nuclear submarine just returned from the North Pole; another person or group trying to cross the Arctic.

    Your report should be organized around some of the following headings: reasons for exploration; difficulties encountered; who financed the voyage; technology used; voyage's importance.

2. There is a great deal of interest in passage through the Arctic today because of the presence of oil and natural gas. Do some research on the potential resources of oil and gas in the Beaufort Sea area. Present an oral or written report to the class on how this is leading to attempts to develop these resources, and to renew interest in the Northwest Passage route.

Be Creative

1. Collect newspaper or magazine headlines or articles on the Canadian North or attempts to make the northwest passage. Report to the class by:
    a) making a collage;
    b) preparing a bulletin board display;
    c) writing a descriptive note;
    d) writing a newspaper account;
    e) providing an oral report.

2. In groups of four, prepare a research folder on "Defence of Canada in the North". Include:
    a) Map — of Polar areas, showing Canada, Alaska, USSR, Northern Europe.
    b) A written note explaining why Canada is interested in defending the Arctic.
    c) An imaginary letter describing moving through the Arctic, and the problems involved.

Can You Recall?

1. Why were whales of such importance to the world before the early 1800s?

2. a) How did the Inuit hunt whales? b) For what purposes did they use each part of the whales?

3. Prepare a report on the Basque whaling station at Red Bay, Labrador, in the 1560s and 1570s, using the following organizers for your report.
    a) map showing whaling station and routes to Basque homeland;
    b) methods of hunting the whales;
    c) description of the process of getting whale oil from whale blubber;
    d) uses of whale oil in Europe.

Research

1. Read the *National Geographic* July 1985 article on "Basque Whalers". Prepare a report on how the Red Bay site was discovered, how they produced whale oil, and how it was transported to Europe.

2. Prepare a report on the Basque people organized under some of the following headings:
    a) the location of the Basque homeland;
    b) the problems of maintaining a separate identity between Spain and France;
    c) some prominent Basque explorers;
    d) the difficulties of the Basque people today as citizens of Spain.

3. *Research topic — Greenpeace Organization*
    Find out what the Greenpeace Organization is. After researching its viewpoint on whales, report to the class its thoughts on a desirable policy on whaling. What do you think a whaling policy should be?

Be Creative

1. Write an imaginary letter from a mother whose son was on a whaling ship that sank.

2. Prepare a diary of a whale hunter who has been at Red Bay, Labrador, for one season.

3. Make a drawing of whale hunting in the 16th century.

4. Prepare a TV interview with a person who has just returned from the whale hunt.

CHAPTER EIGHT / PARTNERS IN TRADE

Units 1. The Search for Fur
2. Port Royal — A French Foothold
3. The Beaver
4. Champlain — Father of New France
5. Clash of Empires — English and Dutch

Can You Recall?

1. Who were the first major fur traders in the world? What effect did their trade have on the supply of furs?
2. Why was North America a good location for the fur trade?
3. The Native Peoples were eager participants in the fur trade. Explain why.
4. List three reasons why Canada had a rich supply of furs.

Ideas for Discussion

1. Work together in small discussion groups. List the possible positive and negative results of wearing clothing made from animal fur.
2. Complete the following sentence: "In my opinion, a love of luxury is/is not wrong because . . . ." Choose one statement. Be prepared to discuss your views with your classmates.

Further Research

1. Find out the meaning of "status symbol". List two status symbols for adults and two for teenagers. What status symbol attracts you the most? Why?
2. Complete brief research on the role of *one* of the following as a symbol: gold, silver, diamonds.
3. How many furs are trapped and sold in Canada today? What is the dollar value of these furs?
4. Read catalogues, brochures, and flyers to find the cost of beaver coats and hats today. You might also find and compare the cost of other luxury furs, such as mink, sable, and fox.

Be Creative

1. Working in small groups, write and perform a brief play about the first meeting of Native Peoples and Cartier.
2. Prepare a collage of the most important fur-bearing animals in Canada. Provide a brief physical description of the animals and their habits with your pictures.

2. Port Royal — a French Foothold (pages 148-151)

3. The Beaver (pages 152-155)

Can You Recall?

Each of the following statements is incorrect. Find the error and then write a correct statement in your notebooks.

1. Fur trading began in 1605 in Canada.
2. The first to trade for furs were soldiers and explorers.
3. France was unable to encourage the fur trade in Canada.
4. The first permanent fur-trading post was established at Tadoussac in 1590.
5. Champlain established "The Order of the Garter".

Ideas for Discussion

1. The French exploration of Canada was largely motivated by simple human greed. Do you agree or disagree? Why?
2. After a brief discussion in small groups, prepare a word collage of your views on winter in Canada.

Further Research

1. Visit the library to research the life and work of Marc Lescarbot.
2. Using your text and other resources, locate the following trading posts on a map: Port Royal, Quebec, Montreal, Tadoussac, Sainte Croix. Do further research on one of these communities today. Prepare an oral and written report for your classmates.
3. Write to Parks Canada for more information on Port Royal. Post any brochures and pictures that you receive.

Be Creative

1. Working from text and library sources, produce a mural depicting different facets of daily life at Port Royal. Some topics might include construction, hunting, fishing, trading, exploration, eating, defending, etc.
2. Organize a survey to discover how your classmates and their families cope with the cold and boredom of winter in Canada.

Can You Recall?

1. What qualities of the Canadian beaver made it suitable for the production of felt hats?
2. "Second-hand" pelts, first worn by the Native Peoples were more valuable than fresh pelts. Carefully explain why this was so?
3. How did the dwindling and expensive supply of Canadian beavers help create "Mad Hatters"?

Ideas for Discussion

1. Do you think it is important to be fashionable? Why or why not?
2. The "Mad Hatters" worked in a very dangerous environment and suffered as a result. Are there jobs today which are hazardous for workers? List as many as you can.
3. What steps can people take to make sure their working environment is safe?

Further Research

1. Find a copy of *Alice in Wonderland* and read the parts dealing with the Mad Hatter. Does knowing the origin of the Hatters change your view of the story?
2. Find and present various pictures showing headgear throughout the ages. Which is your favourite? Why?
3. Investigate the fur trade today. Find Canada's special furs, where they are sold, and how they are used. Is beaver still important in the trade?

**4. Champlain — Father of New France
(pages 156-159)**

**5. Clash of Empires — English and Dutch
(pages 160-163)**

Can You Recall?

1. Why did Champlain abandon the colony at Port Royal?
2. Which people — the Algonquians or the Iroquoians — were most welcoming to the French? Why?
3. Describe the request which the Algonquians and Hurons made of Champlain in 1609. How did Champlain respond? Why?
4. Briefly describe the battle which took place at Lake Champlain in 1609. Why was this battle so important for a) the French, b) the Native Peoples?

Ideas for Discussion

1. List the qualities which you think represent "greatness" in a leader. Was Champlain a "great" leader in your opinion? Explain your answer.
2. How might the weapons of the French affect warfare among the Native Peoples?
3. For debate: Resolved that Champlain was wrong to enter into the wars of the Native Peoples.

Further Research

1. In your library, research the kinds of weapons used by Native Peoples in Canada before the Europeans came. Prepare drawings with brief descriptions. Arrange these in a series of posters.
2. Read more about the lifestyle of the various groups of Native Peoples that Champlain met. Which lifestyle appeals to you the most? Why?
3. Do further research on the tiny settlement which Champlain first built at Quebec. Write a brief description of the post and include pictures.

Be Creative

1. Working in groups, design and complete a newspaper detailing the life and character of Samuel de Champlain. Select a suitable masthead for your paper. Be sure to include appropriate headlines, news events, illustrations, cartoons, interviews, correspondents' reports, advertisements, letters to the editor, and other suitable features.

Can You Recall?

1. On a map, locate early English settlements in North America, e.g., Jamestown and Cupids Bay.
2. Why did the English attack French settlements in Acadia?
3. State the two main reasons for English interest in Newfoundland.
4. In which part of North America did the Dutch settle? Be specific.
5. List the factors which made life very difficult for French fur traders at this time. Which factor was most important? Why?

Ideas for Discussion

1. Which people, the English, French, Dutch, or Native Peoples, had the best claim to possession of North America? Why?
2. The use of tobacco has proved to be tragic for many people. Work in groups to list as many negative features of tobacco use as possible. Share your ideas with the entire class.

Further Research

1. Research the life and voyages of Henry Hudson. Present your information as a trading card, with picture on one side and printed notes on the other.
2. Read further about Samuel Argall's attacks against the French in Acadia.
3. Visit the library to find illustrations depicting life in Jamestown.
4. Try to discover the various fishing methods used by the English at this time. Summarize these methods in a brief note. Include drawings or diagrams.

Be Creative

1. Pretend that Champlain and Hudson *did* meet in the Lake Champlain region in 1609. Write a brief record of what they might possibly have said to each other. Present this imaginary dialogue to the rest of the class.
2. Organize a special "Hotline" show with Marie La Tour, Charles La Tour, and Charles D'Aulnay as guests. Students selected to be the above people should do some background reading before the show. The rest of the class should prepare questions and comments. They should be prepared to "phone in" on the day of the show.

CHAPTER NINE / DISPLACED PERSONS

1. New England (pages 164-167)

Units 1. New England
2. New France — A Tiny Population
3. New France — The Vast Empire
4. The Church in the Wilderness
5. Displacement of the Native Peoples

Can You Recall?

1. In one or two brief sentences identify each of the following: enclosure, Puritan, *Mayflower*.
2. Explain the Puritans' decision to leave England and head for North America.
3. What evidence is there that the English colonies in North America were soon "booming"?
4. Rank in order the following communities in terms of population from largest to smallest: French, Dutch, English. Explain their sizes.

Ideas for Discussion

1. Name at least three places in the world today where people still struggle over religion. Briefly describe the reasons for this struggle for *one* of these places. Why are religious conflicts often so bloody and difficult to solve?
2. Brainstorm as many positive results of living in a multicultural society as you can. Rank order the five major advantages and be prepared to explain your selection.

Further Research

1. Find out how people travelled to North America from Europe around the year 1600. Make a list of the main dangers and difficulties facing people crossing the ocean.
2. Locate a picture of the *Mayflower* and read a brief account of the voyage of the Pilgrims. Pretend you were a Pilgrim on the *Mayflower*. Write a brief account of your voyage.

Be Creative

1. Write short poems about enclosure and pass them around the classroom. If possible, illustrate your work.
2. Poll your class to determine the number of languages spoken and/or understood by your classmates. Create a language mural of several common phrases in the various languages.

2. New France — a Tiny Population (pages 168-173)

Can You Recall?

1. Explain why so few French people emigrated to colonies in North America.
2. Name the main duties and rights of the seigneurs and the censitaires.
3. In a brief paragraph, show how the French interest in the fur trade restricted population growth in New France.

Ideas For Discussion

1. For debate: Resolved that the trapping of animals for their pelts is morally wrong.
2. If you were the French king, how would you have increased the population of New France?

Further Research

1. Research the population growth in New France and New England from 1608 to 1700. Present your findings in table or graph form.
2. Find out more about the beliefs and history of the Huguenots by consulting encyclopedias in your library. Make a brief report.
3. Describe the main pattern of living on a seigneury and look for other patterns.

Be Creative

1. Re-create the excitement and activities of the Montreal fur fair. Have classmates play traders, soldiers, trappers, Native Peoples, etc. Set up trading booths and bargain pelts (old fur coats, hats, etc.) for European products (tools, bowls, blankets).
2. Design a poster advertising the fur fairs at Montreal or Tadoussac. Select the best design and award a prize.

3. New France — the Vast Empire (pages 174-177)

Can You Recall?

1. Draw and label a picture of a beaver lodge. Explain why it is easy to catch beaver.
2. In a paragraph, describe the job and lifestyle of the coureur-de-bois sent to live among the Native Peoples.
3. Draw and label a map of the Great Lakes area which the French had explored by the 1630s.

Ideas For Discussion

1. Brainstorm the positive and negative results of Europeans living among the Native Peoples. Then rank order each list from most important to least important.
2. Imagine you are a French explorer meeting a group of Native People for the first time. Write a short speech you would make to these people. Present this speech to the class.

Further Research

1. Using the library, find examples of maps drawn by early French explorers. Compare these maps with present-day maps. Note two or three major similarities and differences. Post the maps side by side.
2. Research further into the lives of Brûlé and Nicollet. Present your findings in a brief, illustrated report.
3. Read excerpts from Champlain's journals. Summarize one entry in your own words. Place your work on a postcard to be sent from Champlain to his wife Hélène, in France.

Be Creative

1. Design coins or stamps to commemorate the exploits of an early explorer, such as Brûlé, Nicollet, or Champlain. Organize a class competition to judge the best designs.

4. The Church in the Wilderness
(pages 178-181)

Can You Recall?

1. Match the terms in Group A with the suitable description in Group B.

Group A	Group B
a) Ville-Marie	i) Black Robes
b) Huron Carol	ii) Catherine Tekakwitha
c) Lily of The Mohawks	iii) Montreal
d) Sainte-Marie-Among-the-Hurons	iv) hymn composed by Jesuits for Native People
e) Society of Jesus	v) Jesuit mission in Ontario
	vi) Maisonneuve's settlement

2. Describe two social institutions developed by religious orders in New France.

3. To which group of Native People did the Jesuits devote most attention? Why?

4. Describe Maisonneuve's dreams for Ville-Marie.

Ideas for Discussion

1. In small groups, select the *five* most important characteristics for a missionary in New France during the 1700s. Explain why these characteristics are so important. Share your findings with the class.

2. If you were a Huron, how might you have reacted to the arrival of the Black Robes? What do you feel was the most suitable response? Why?

3. For debate: Resolved that people of one faith should not try to convert people of another faith.

Further Research

1. Collect pictures of the first churches, hospitals, and schools of New France. Organize these in a photo album and write brief captions for them. You may have to draw, trace, or photocopy some of your illustrations.

2. Research the religion of the Huron people. Prepare a brief summary of their key beliefs and practices. (See Chapter Two, Unit 4 of this book.)

Be Creative

1. Pretend that you are a Black Robe working in Huronia. Write two or three entries in your journal. Describe your activities, thoughts, fears, and observations.

2. Have someone play the Huron Carol on piano or guitar and sing it as a group. Discuss your reactions to the words and melody. How might the music affect the people at Saint-Marie-Among-the-Hurons?

5. Displacement of the Native Peoples
(pages 182-183)

Ideas for Discussion

1. For debate: Resolved that the fur trade enriched only the Europeans and destroyed the Native Peoples. Working in small groups, prepare a list of arguments for and against the above resolution.

2. Brainstorm a list of the positive and negative results of European contact for the Native Peoples. Decide whether contact was generally good or bad. Share your views with one other classmate.

Further Research

1. Research and briefly describe some of the diseases brought to North America by the Europeans. Which diseases are still serious threats today?

2. Consult daily newspapers and clip articles about Native Peoples issues today. Read and discuss these clippings in a current events discussion.

Be Creative

1. Assume you are members of a Native tribe in New France. Hold a meeting to discuss the arrival and spread of the Europeans. Make speeches telling your views. Offer some ideas about how to deal with the situation. At the end, take a vote on the actions proposed.

2. Invite a speaker from a Native People's organization to speak to your class about issues facing today's Native Peoples.

Units 1. War among the Native Peoples
2. The Iroquois Offensive
3. The Sun King and New France
4. Radisson and Groseilliers: Under Two Flags
5. The French Drive into the Interior

1. War Among the Native Peoples (pages 184-187)

Can You Recall?

Identify the following statements as true or false. If false, rewrite the statement so that it is true. Copy all "true" statements into your notebook.

1. To control the fur trade, the Iroquois decided to wipe out their Huron rivals.   T   F
2. The Dutch provided few muskets to the Iroquois.   T   F
3. The Jesuits accidentally weakened the Hurons by bringing European diseases.   T   F
4. Few Hurons blamed the "Black Robes" for their problems.   T   F
5. The Jesuits were scarcely touched by the Iroquois raids.   T   F
6. Building empires was a cruel business in New France.   T   F

Ideas for Discussion

1. Was there any possibility of peace between the Huron and Iroquois, once the Europeans arrived? Working in threes, listen to each other's reaction to the above question. Hold a brief discussion and try to arrive at a group response to be shared with classmates.
2. Does "empire-building" among nations have to lead to war? Examine this question from the viewpoint of the history you have studied.

Further Research

1. Find and read other excerpts from the *Jesuit Relations*. Place your excerpts and those of your classmates in a special binder with an appropriate and attractive cover. Select students to read different excerpts out loud on a daily basis as you study this unit.

Be Creative

1. Design posters urging peace between the Huron and Iroquois. Employ suitable symbols, illustrations, and slogans. Divide the class into Huron and Iroquois and hold a special conference to discuss ways of bringing peace to your warring peoples.
2. Working from pictures found in library books and texts, create a miniature model of a Huron or Iroquois village.
   Build models of longhouses, palisades, crop fields, etc. Invite other classes to come in to view and discuss your work.

2. The Iroquois Offensive (pages 188-191)

Can You Recall?

1. For what reasons were the Iroquois able to increase their attacks on New France?
2. Explain why Ville-Marie was most likely to suffer Iroquois attack.
3. List the important contributions made by religious women to life in New France. Whom do you think was most important? Why?

Ideas for Discussion

1. Complete the following statements in your own words: The world will be free of war when .... Be prepared to defend your statement orally.
2. What kinds of feelings would the French-Iroquois Wars create in the combatants themselves? After a brief discussion, pick out and print all these words. Then make a collage of these words.

Further Research

1. Do some further reading on the French-Iroquois Wars. Then make a chart showing the strengths and weaknesses of the Iroquois and the French. Which side had the greatest power? Why?
2. Make a time chart indicating five of the major events in French-Iroquois relations. You should start with Cartier's visit to the St. Lawrence (1534). Your chart should include the following headings: Date, Event, Brief Description of Event, Importance.

Be Creative

1. Debate: Resolved that the Iroquois were entirely right in seeking to defeat the French.
2. Organize a Remembrance Day service for those who fell in wars between Europeans and Native Peoples. You should include prayers, music, and suitable religious symbols.

3. The Sun King and New France (pages 192-197)

Can You Recall?

1. a) Describe how the "Sun King" viewed the French Empire.
   b) What specific steps did Louis XIV take to deal with the Iroquois?
2. List three things Jean Talon did to make New France more self-supporting.
3. Increasing the population of New France was important for French officials. What did they do to boost the colony's tiny population? Were they successful?
4. Give three reasons why women were vital to the future of the colony.

Ideas for Discussion

1. Working in small groups, prepare a list of positive and negative qualities of Louis XIV. In your opinion, was he a great monarch? Explain your answer.
2. Offer reasons for and against the French burning of Iroquois villages and crops. Should there be limits to military action during wartime? Explain?

Further Research

1. Research further into the history of the Carignan-Salières regiment in Canada. Prepare a brief written report using the following headings: Campaigns, Uniforms, Weapons. Provide illustrations with your report.
2. Produce a biography card for Jean-Baptiste Colbert and Jean Talon. One side of your card should have an illustration; the other should provide important details of your subject's life. Possible headings could include: Early Life, Career, Quotations, Importance.

Be Creative

1. Pretend you are Jean Talon. Write a one-page letter to Louis XIV. Indicate the characteristics most desired in women who would come to live in the colony.
2. Organize an interview with the Sun King as the guest. Select a panel of students to prepare "tough" questions for the Sun King. After the panel asks its questions, invite questions and comments from the audience (class). Topics which might be discussed include France's Wars, Finances, New France.

**4. Radisson and Groseilliers:
Under Two Flags (pages 198-203)**

Can You Recall?

1. Match the items in column A with the items in column B. One description does not fit at all.

A	B
i) *Nonsuch*	a) Groseilliers
ii) Radisson	b) Prince Rupert
iii) Coureurs-de-bois	c) great northern sea
iv) Hudson Bay	d) unofficial fur traders
v) Hudson's Bay Co.	e) English sailing vessel

2. Why did Radisson and Groseilliers first join forces with the English?

3. Why was Hudson Bay of great interest to the English and the French?

Ideas for Discussion

1. Radisson and Groseilliers shifted their loyalties between England and France. In your opinion, were they justified in doing this? Explain fully. What do their actions reveal about their values (things which they prized)?

2. Prepare and present a brief speech which Radisson might have given to attract English investors to his schemes.

Further Research

1. Research in some of Radisson's journals. Read interesting selections to your classmates.

2. Locate a picture of the rebuilt *Nonsuch*. Note the important dimensions of the ship. Make a diagram of the ship and label the various parts of the vessel.

3. Trace the journeys of Radisson and Groseilliers on a large map of North America. Further information may be found in a library or classroom source book.

Be Creative

1. Assume that Radisson and Groseilliers were captured by the French. Organize a trial on the charge of treason. Appoint a jury, prosecutor, defence attorney, judges, clerks, witnesses, etc. Decide whether or not the adventurers were guilty of the charges.

5. The French Drive to the Interior (pages 204-207)

Can You Recall?

1. Carefully explain three reasons why the English proved to be such dangerous rivals to the French in the 1670s.

2. Describe what Frontenac did to counter the English challenge. Do you feel this was a sound response?

3. Prepare a brief note describing the work of La Salle. Comment on the importance of his contribution to the exploration of North America.

Ideas for Discussion

1. Good leadership depends on several important qualities. List as many of these qualities as you can. Which qualities did La Salle possess? Which qualities did he lack? On the basis of your choices, was La Salle a good leader?

Further Research

1. Using other research sources and this text, prepare a map showing the routes of Marquette, Jolliet, and La Salle. Indicate major river systems, lakes, and trading posts.

2. Make copies of illustrations (maps, pictures, etc.) from the travels of Jolliet and Marquette and La Salle. Organize these illustrations into an Art Gallery of French Exploration. Provide brief captions to explain your illustrations. Your gallery should also be set up in chronological order.

Be Creative

1. Write a brief epitaph to be placed on a tombstone or monument which you have designed for La Salle.

2. Keep a diary for La Salle during his last expedition. Write what you think would have been his thoughts, hopes, and fears during this challenging time.

CHAPTER ELEVEN / A BALANCE OF POWER

1. European Wars (pages 208-209)

Units 1. European Wars
2. North American Wars
3. D'Iberville: New France's Greatest Warrior
4. Louisiana
5. Fortress Louisbourg

Can You Recall?

1. Name the three important ruling families of Europe and the countries which they governed.
2. For what reason did English Protestants invite William of Orange to take the throne of England?

Ideas for Discussion

1. In small groups, brainstorm a list of methods of government other than rule by a monarch. Which method has the support of the most members of your group? Why? Share your findings with the rest of the class.

Further Research

1. Visit the library to find pictures of crowns, royal crests, flags, and other symbols of the Stuart, Habsburg, and Bourbon royal families. Reproduce some of these symbols and post them around the room. Find the meanings of parts of these symbols.

2. North American Wars (pages 210-213)

Can You Recall?

1. Describe how Frontenac responded to the English demand to surrender at Quebec. What was the result of this encounter?
2. Write a summary of the achievements of Governor Frontenac.

Ideas for Discussion

1. In wartime, people often commit brutal acts of terror. In groups, prepare a word collage of brutal acts from any wars, past or present. Discuss why ordinary people are capable of terrifying deeds during wartime.
2. A hero can be defined as "one who is fearless and acts well at all times". Was Governor Frontenac a hero? Refer to his career to find information which supports your view. Be prepared to discuss your views orally with your classmates.

Further Research

1. Read further about the Lachine Massacre. Organize your findings in a brief "news report" to be "broadcast" to the class.
2. Find pictures and descriptions of the uniforms and weapons of the Troupes de la Marine. Present your findings in a series of captioned drawings or prints.

Be Creative

1. Pretend you are Governor Frontenac and write a military report to Louis XIV. Describe the actions of the English and Iroquois. Explain how you are dealing with them. Make any requests which you feel would be suitable.
2. Write your own song or poem about Frontenac's famous and successful defence of Quebec. Perform it for the class.
3. Design a recruiting poster urging men to join les Troupes de la Marine.

3. D'Iberville: New France's Greatest Warrior (pages 214-217)

Can You Recall?

1. Describe how the French responded to the growth of English forts on Hudson Bay.
2. Prepare a brief biographical note of d'Iberville. Your note should include information under the following headings: Early Life, Hudson Bay Battles, Warfare in Acadia, The Last Years.
3. What specific qualities did d'Iberville possess that earned him the title "New France's Greatest Warrior"?

Ideas for Discussion

1. Brainstorm a list of reasons for conflict between individuals. Which of these reasons can also result in war between nations? Which reason for conflict is the most serious in your opinion? Why?
2. Working in groups, try to find or make a definition for "bravery". Does your definition apply to d'Iberville? Are you aware of other "brave" people? Who? Do you know any "brave" people personally? Describe their bravery.

Further Research

1. Look over maps of the fortifications and trading posts on Hudson Bay in the 1690s. Draw both French and English positions on a map of North America.
2. Look at a modern map of Newfoundland and find as many French place names as you can. Write these names in a list. In which areas of the province do the French appear to be concentrated?

4. Louisiana (pages 218-219)

Can You Recall?

1. Explain the key reason for Louis XIV's interest in Louisiana.
2. Describe the thinking behind the French decision to build a) New Orleans, b) Fort Détroit. Find these on your map.
3. Louis XIV placed much hope on the success of his chain of forts along the Mississippi River. What did he hope to gain from this action?

Further Research

1. Investigate further the career of Antoine de la Mothe Cadillac and prepare a one-page biography card. Focus mainly on his activities in North America.

Be Creative

1. Visit local travel agents and gather brochures and posters on Louisiana. Write to tourism bureaus for the State of Louisiana and major cities, such as New Orleans and Baton Rouge. Mount a display of the state's major sites of interest. Place special emphasis on French areas of Louisiana.

5. Fortress Louisbourg (pages 220-223)

Can You Recall?

1. List the territories lost by France in the Treaty of Utrecht.
2. Louisbourg was a massive and expensive fortification. For what purposes was it constructed by the French?

Ideas for Discussion

1. How would the Acadians have felt when they learned they had been put under control of the English? What do you think would have troubled them the most? Explain.

Further Research

1. Find out other terms of the Treaty of Utrecht. Which country, England or France, appears to be the victor? Why?
2. Research further into the history and culture of either the Micmac or Abenaki nations. Present a brief illustrated report.
3. Write to Parks Canada at Louisbourg (Cape Breton, Nova Scotia) and request photos and brochures.

   a) Make a collage for your bulletin board
   or
   b) Write a report with supporting illustrations describing the fortress today.

Be Creative

1. Assume you are an Acadian farmer who has just learned that his land has become a part of English territory. Compose a letter which you think he might have written to the new English governor. Express the hopes and fears he might hold for the future. Express any requests which you feel might have been made.

CHAPTER TWELVE / THE FALL OF NEW FRANCE

Units 1. The Great War for Empire
2. 1740's — The War Continues
3. The Seven Years War Begins
4. Expulsion of the Acadians
5. The Fall of New France, 1759

1. The Great War for Empire (pages 224-225)

Can You Recall?

1. France and Britain struggled over many products during the War of the Austrian Succession. Match the product on the left with the geographic area on the right.

Product	Geographic Area
i) Fish	A) East Indies
ii) Spices	B) East Coast of Canada
iii) Sugar	C) North America
iv) Tobacco	D) Caribbean

Ideas for Discussion

1. In your opinion, is it worth fighting over products like fish, sugar, and spices? Are there any products today that are worth the risking of lives? Explain why.

Further Research

1. Visit a local supermarket and view the fish, sugar, and spices mentioned in this unit. How expensive are these products today? Which are used by your family? Which countries supply these products today?

2. 1740s – The War Continues (pages 226-227) **3. The Seven Years' War Begins (pages 228-229)**

Can You Recall?

1. Describe the reasons why La Vérendrye sent his sons to the "Mountains of Bright Stones".

Ideas for Discussion

1. In groups, prepare a list of reasons for New France's policy of territorial growth. Try to present a series of alternatives to expansion that the French might have tried. Which alternative does your group prefer? Why?

Further Research

1. Read further about the remarkable La Vérendrye family. Prepare a family tree naming other family members and their explorations and discoveries.
2. Select *one* of the French forts. Do research on this fort, and prepare a report to include
   a) a map showing its location;
   b) a drawing or picture;
   c) a description of the fort and its purpose.

Be Creative

Design your own plan for a fort during the period 1700-1760 in North America. Carefully consider the climate and the weapons available at this time. Make sure your design is neatly drawn and clearly labelled. Give your fort a name.

Can You Recall?

1. In a brief sentence or two identify each of the following. Explain their importance related to migration and settlement.
   a) Appalachian Mountains;
   b) Cumberland Gap;
   c) Ohio Valley.
2. Locate all of the above on a sketch map. Also show the position of New France, New England, and Louisiana.
3. Explain why both French and English desired the Ohio Valley.
4. Describe the results of the violent clash between English and French in the Ohio lands.

Ideas for Discussion

1. With a partner, discuss which nation — England or France — had the best claim to the Ohio country. Draw up a list of arguments for each side. Make a final decision as to which side had the best claim.
2. The Ohio Valley was a "hot spot" that eventually set off a major war between England and France. Make a list of "hot spots" in the world today. Which countries would be involved if these "hot spots" exploded into open war?

Further Research

1. Find pictures showing settlers moving through the Cumberland Gap or settling the Ohio Valley. After analyzing this material, write a one-page report describing the steps of settlement. You might include a description of the settlers, their transportation, their work, etc.

4. Expulsion of the Acadians (pages 230-233)

Can You Recall?

1. Prepare a brief summary in your own words of the Acadian tragedy. Your report should have separate paragraphs devoted to the following:
   a) the reasons for the English decision to deport the Acadians;
   b) the lands to which the Acadians were sent;
   c) why the deportation was so hard on the Acadians.
2. Briefly identify Gabriel and Evangeline. In what famous poem are they featured? Who was the author of this work?

Ideas for Discussion

1. Choose a partner and discuss the Acadian deportation. One person should represent the views of the Acadians; the other should represent the British viewpoint. Note the most important points raised by each side.
2. As the Acadians prepared to board English ships for exile, they must have had worries. Jot down a list of these "probable" worries. Rank order these worries.
3. If you were an Acadian, how would you have responded to British orders to pack up and leave? After a class discussion, compose a letter to British authorities stating your feelings and intended actions.

Further Research

1. Find a copy of Longfellow's poem "Evangeline" and read it. Briefly state your impressions of the poem.

Be Creative

1. Create your own story of "The Acadian Deportation". Working in groups, present your legend in the form of a short play.
2. Working in groups of four or five, prepare a "jackdaw" on the Deportation of the Acadians. Your jackdaw should be well-designed and attractively illustrated. Each jackdaw should contain 10 items and include the following:
   a) a *map* showing the Acadian lands in Canada's Maritimes;
   b) some "lost" letters or diaries recording the thoughts of the Acadians during this period (written by you);
   c) pictures of Acadian homes, farms, clothing, and other items which your imagination can suggest.

5. The Fall of New France (pages 234-239)

Can You Recall?

1. Explain how Prussian soldiers in Europe helped defeat France in North America.
2. Wolfe was victorious in 1759. Carefully explain the reasons behind the British victory. Which, in your opinion, was most important? Why?
3. Why did the French government prefer Guadeloupe to Canada?

Ideas for Discussion

1. Was the outcome of the Battle of the Plains of Abraham a great tragedy, a noble victory, or both? Discuss from the point of view of a) French habitant, b) British soldier, c) yourself.
2. If you were Montcalm, how might you have handled the arrival of British forces on the Plains of Abraham? What orders would you have given to those under your command?
3. "Canada was never fully appreciated by France." Discuss this statement.

Further Research

1. Do further research on a) Montcalm; b) Wolfe. Write a report on your research. Conclude with your assessment of whether or not each was a good general.
2. Study maps clearly showing French and English positions during the Siege of Quebec. In your opinion, which army held the best positions? Why?

Be Creative

1. Organize a TV "You Are There" special on the Battle of Quebec. Have roving war correspondents report "live" from the Battle of the Plains of Abraham. You might include the following in your "broadcast":
   a) an anchor desk to introduce the various parts of the telecast
   b) correspondents to interview Wolfe and Montcalm
   c) reporters to describe the battle from the French and British lines
   d) reports from field hospitals
   e) interviews with women and children within the walls of Quebec
   f) commercial breaks
   Present your programme live or have it taped and then played on a colour TV.
2. Design a fitting memorial for Generals Wolfe and Montcalm. Whatever structure you design, include a brief inscription.

CHAPTER THIRTEEN / THE PARTING OF THE WAYS

Units 1. Quebec in the 1760's
2. "No Taxation Without Representation"
3. Conflict over the Ohio Valley
4. Divided Opinions in the Thirteen Colonies
5. The Loyalists

1. Quebec in the 1760s (pages 240-243)

Can You Recall?

1. Explain at least three ways in which Quebec was different from the other British Colonies in North America.
2. Briefly describe three of the groups that made up Quebec society — the seigneurs, habitants, voyageurs.
3. Make a sketch of how land was divided in the seigneuries. Explain why it usually consisted of long strips stretching to the river.

Ideas for Discussion

1. Explain what Governor Guy Carleton meant when he said "It seems as if this country must, to the end of time, be peopled by the Canadian race." Do you agree?
2. There is much more written about *men* in early Quebec than about *women*. Why might this be? Is this still true today?

Research

1. Research about the different groups of Quebec society (seigneurs, habitants, voyageurs, clergy). Select the one you would have preferred to be. Write a report describing this group. Explain why you would have preferred to be in this group.
2. Research about the role of women in Quebec. Write a report on their role, or on a famous woman of the period.

Be creative

1. Research the life of a seigneur, a habitant (male or female), or a voyageur. Write a letter or diary entry describing your life in Quebec in the 1760s, to a friend in France. Your letter might begin: Dear __ , As you know, the English have now arrived. Although many things have changed, life goes on much as before ___

2. No Taxation Without Representation
(pages 244-247)

Can You Recall?
1. In one or two sentences explain what each of the following meant. How did each contribute to the American Revolution?
   Stamp Act - 1765
   Townshend Duties - 1767
   Boston Massacre - 1770
   Boston Tea Party - 1773
   Intolerable Acts - 1774

Research and Creative Response
1. Find out more about the life of one of the following patriots of the Thirteen Colonies:
   -Patrick Henry
   -Samuel Adams
   -Tom Paine
   -Thomas Jefferson

   Present his grievance to the rest of the class. Use a poster, a proclamation, a letter to a newspaper, an interview, or a speech.
2. Summarize the grievances of the colonists towards Britain. Organize these into a document of protest. Present this written document to the "Governor".

3. Conflict Over the Ohio Valley
(pages 248-251)

Can You Recall?
1. Explain why the Indians in the Ohio Valley welcomed the French, but were opposed to the English.
2. What was Pontiac's Rebellion? Why did it lead the British to create an "Indian Territory" in the Ohio Valley?
3. Complete the following chart in your workbook, under the heading: Events Leading to the American Revolution.

Event	What Happened	Results
Pontiac's Rebellion		
Creation of Indian Territory		
Quebec Act		
Lexington and Concord		
Declaration of Independence		

Explain how each event in the chart helped to *cause* the next listed event.

For Research and Discussion
1. The American soldiers frequently fought in small units rather than in large armies. This would later be described as a form of "guerrilla warfare". (From Spanish "guerra"; means "little war".)

   Find an example where guerrilla warfare is being carried on today. Research how the local forces fight against invaders. In what ways is this type of warfare similar to that of the American colonists fighting the British?

Be Creative
1. Draw a picture of a typical British soldier and an American colonist.
2. Prepare a poster or proclamation showing
   a) a rebel calling on the colonists to rebel
   b) a British official asking the people to support the British

4. Divided Opinions in the Thirteen Colonies (pages 252-255)

Can You Recall?

1. Explain why not all of the British colonists supported the revolution:
   a) colonists in Newfoundland
   b) colonists in Nova Scotia
   c) colonists in Quebec
2. Why did some colonists within the Thirteen Colonies not support the Revolution?
3. Explain how different groups within Quebec were pleased by the Quebec Act, therefore refusing to support the Revolution.
4. a) Explain the terms - Loyalist
                           - Patriots
   b) Why did many Loyalists choose to leave the Thirteen Colonies and move to British North America?

Research

1. Do research on the United Empire Loyalists today. What are some of their attitudes? What impact did they have on the development of British North America and Canada?

Be Creative

1. With a partner, prepare an interview with a Loyalist. In your interview you might explain why you left the colonies and chose to move to Canada. *or*
2. With a partner, do research and prepare a TV interview with one of the leaders of the American Revolution. You might choose Patrick Henry, Samuel Adams, Tom Paine, or George Washington. You could also choose any other person you discover in your research. Present your interview to the class.

5. The Loyalists (pages 256-261)

Can You Recall?

1. Identify the two francophone groups involved in the American Revolution. Explain why they were on opposite sides.
2. What assistance was provided to the Loyalists when they arrived in British North America?
3. Explain how the arrival of the Loyalists led to
   a) the creation of New Brunswick;
   b) the creation of Upper and Lower Canada.

Ideas for Discussion

1. The Loyalists are credited with re-inforcing much of our British attitudes. Which attitudes did they bring that have affected our British heritage?

Research

1. Do further research on one of the following groups of Loyalists:
   a) Black Loyalists in the Maritimes
   b) Six Nations settlement of the Grand River
   c) German Loyalists in Upper Canada and Nova Scotia

Be creative

In a group of four or five students, prepare a Jackdaw on the Loyalists. Your folder should include:
a) a *map* showing the migration route and areas of Loyalist settlement
b) *letters* or diaries of several Loyalists describing their move
c) a *newspaper account* describing aspects of Loyalist migration or settlement
d) a *poster* advertising land for the Loyalists, or indicating what goods they would receive
e) a *picture* of the Loyalists
Place the material in a folder that you have illustrated.
Prepare an oral and visual presentation for the rest of your class.

CHAPTER FOURTEEN / STRUGGLE FOR SURVIVAL

Units 1. Causes of the War of 1812
2. The War of 1812
3. The Northwest Company vs the Bay
4. Struggle for the West
5. Struggle for the Pacific Coast

1. Causes of the War of 1812 (pages 262-265)

Can You Recall?

1. Explain the connection of each of the following to the background of the war of 1812: Napoleon, Thomas Jefferson, press-gangs, continental blockade.
2. In 1812, what advantages did the U.S. have over the colonists in Upper Canada?
3. How did the British wars with Napoleon help to bring about the invasion of Canada?
4. What was Upper Canada like in the early 1800s?
   a) town life
   b) pioneer (rural) life

Ideas for Discussion

1. What did Jefferson mean when he said that "the annexation of Canada . . . will be a mere matter of marching." Why were the Americans so confident of their success in this war?

Research

1. Do further research on either John Graves Simcoe or Elizabeth Simcoe. What was their contribution to life in Upper Canada?
2. The "War Hawks" of the United States supported the invasion of Upper Canada. Research who they were, and why they were opposed to the British in North America.

2. The War of 1812 (pages 266-271)

Can You Recall?

1. Construct a chart on the War of 1812. For each of the following:
   a) identify or explain the person or event, b) give the date, c) tell what happened, and d) its importance in the war.
   Places - Queenston Heights
   - York
   - Chateauguay
   - Washington
   People - Isaac Brock
   - Chief Tecumseh
   - Laura Secord
   - Charles de Salaberry

Ideas for Discussion

1. The Americans thought that the invasion would be simply "a matter of marching". How do you account for the fact that the American invasion failed?

Research

1. Do some research on the War of 1812 using an American textbook or source. Is their description of the war different from ours? How? How do you account for this?
2. Do research on one of: General Brock, Laura Secord, Chief Tecumseh, Charles de Salaberry. You should focus on their background, their achievement, and its importance in the War of 1812.

Be Creative

1. Draw a poster to rally Canadian support for the war in 1812.
2. In groups of two, prepare an interview with one of the individuals involved in the war. Present your TV interview to the class.
3. In groups of three or four, prepare a jackdaw folder on the War of 1812. Your folder should include:
   a) a map showing the key battles of the war
   b) a newspaper account of one or more battles in the war
   c) a diary entry from an individual in the war
   d) a letter from an American soldier, part of the invading army
   e) any other items you wish to include.
   Present your information in a folder with a cover design relating to the war.

3. The North West Company vs The Bay (pages 272-275)

Can You Recall?

1. a) Make up a chart for these explorers of the North West Company:
   - Alexander Mackenzie
   - Simon Fraser
   b) For each one, indicate the route of his voyage, and the importance of his exploration.
2. On a map of British North America:
   - trace the voyages of Mackenzie and Fraser;
   - locate the main Hudson's Bay fur forts;
   - indicate the fur routes of the North West Company and the Hudson's Bay Company.

Research

1. Do research on the explorations of Alexander Mackenzie or Simon Fraser.
2. One of the outstanding explorers for the Hudson's Bay Company was Samuel Hearne. Research his explorations. What was their importance to the "Men of the Bay"?

Be Creative

1. After further research on one of these explorers, write a letter or diary. Record what it was like to explore the difficult and unexplored lands of the West.

4. Struggle for the West (pages 276-279)

Can You Recall?

1. Identify and tell why the following were important in the growth of the West:
   - Lord Selkirk
   - Red River Colony, 1812
   - the Métis
   - Marie-Anne Lagimodière
   - The Northwest trade routes
   - Seven Oaks Massacre, 1816
   - Merger of the Northwest Company and the Hudson's Bay Company, 1821.

For Discussion

1. After reading "Uses of the Buffalo", prepare a written or oral petition to the Governor of the Selkirk Settlement from a Métis or Plains Indian explaining why settlement on the Prairies would destroy the way of life of the Native Peoples.

Creative Research — a Group Activity

You are residents of the Selkirk settlement on Red River, in the year 1812. You are going to publish a newspaper for your colony.
- Form groups of five or six students.
- Examine a modern newspaper and note the various sections (i.e., front page, headlines, pictures, news reports, foreign news, advertisements, editorials, letters to the editor, cartoons, social news, etc.).
- Give out assignments to each reporter (it may help to appoint an *editor* to be in charge of the organization).
- Research and write your reports about the colony. They might include a description of events in the colony in that year, reports on the trip from Scotland, letters to the editor, editorials, editorial cartoons, social events, advertisements, etc.
- Assign foreign news reporters to discover what was going on in other parts of the world in 1812 (i.e., in other parts of British North America, and in Europe).
- Add suitable pictures or cartoons.
- When you have completed your report, have it edited by another reporter in your group.
- Re-write or type your report in presentable copy.
- Share your newspaper with others in the class.

5. Struggle for the Pacific Coast (pages 280-283)

Can You Recall?

1. Construct a chart about exploration of the Pacific coast. You might use these headings as organizers for your chart: Name, Nationality, Year, Area Explored, Importance. Your chart should include:
   Vitus Bering, James Cook, George Vancouver.

Ideas for Discussion

1. Divide the class in half. One half will represent the European explorers. The other half will represent the Native Peoples of the west coast. Have a discussion (or debate) on who had the rights to the lands of the Pacific coast.
2. After the class discussion, write a report which should include three paragraphs (or sections):
   a) The European claim to the Pacific coast
   b) The Native Peoples' rights to the Pacific coast
   c) *Your opinion* as to who had the rights. Give reasons for your opinion.
3. The question of rights to land is often an issue today. Discuss any recent issues over land ownership or land use in British Columbia.

For Creative Research

1. Do research on one of the people or groups involved in the struggle for the Pacific coast.
   Present your findings in the form of
   . a written report
   . an interview
   . a picture or cartoon

Units 1. The Great Migration
2. Impact of the Great Migration
3. Unrest in Upper and Lower Canada
4. Rebellions of 1837
5. Emergence of British Columbia

1. The Great Migration (pages 284-287)

Can You Recall?

1. Describe each of the following. Explain how each either increased or decreased immigration to Canada:
   - Steam Power
   - The Industrial Revolution
   - The Napoleonic Wars
   - The Potato Famine in Ireland
2. List the main sources of immigration to Canada in the period after 1815.

For research and Discussion

1. Do some research on the potato famine of 1846-47 in Ireland. Why do some people feel that the roots of the present conflict in Ireland go back to 1846 or even beyond?

2. Select a newspaper item on a recent event related to immigration. Write a news report on this item in your own words. Describe what happened and try to explain why it happened. Give your opinion on the likely consequences of this event.

3. Create a bulletin board on the topic "Immigration Today". Record examples of successes and difficulties of recent immigrants.

4. Write a report comparing immigration today with immigration in the early 1800s. Try to show problems that still exist for immigrants. Also show improved conditions that they find.   *or*

   Do a personal history (or genealogy) of your family. Tell the story of how and why your family came to Canada.

2. Impact of the Great Migration
(pages 288-293)

Can You Recall?
1. a) Which group of settlers made up British North America before 1815?
   b) Which new groups arrived after 1815? How did this change the population?
2. On a blank map of British North America, locate at least seven towns that existed by 1850.

Ideas for Discussion
1. In groups of three or four, make lists of the
   —3 greatest difficulties facing pioneers;
   —3 greatest advantages or opportunities for pioneers;
   —3 greatest difficulties of living in your community today;
   —3 greatest advantages of living in your community today.
   After exchanging views with other groups, make composite lists.
2. Have a class debate: Resolved that it was better (worse) living in a pioneer community than living here today.

Research
1. In groups of two, research the life and writings of Susanna Moodie, Catharine Parr Traill, or another pioneer settler. Prepare an interview with this pioneer. Role-play your interview for the class.

Be Creative
1. In groups of four students, create a folder about life in pioneer times. Your folder should include:
   a) a map of areas settled by pioneers in the early 1800s;
   b) a poster advertising land in British North America, for settlers from Britain;
   c) a letter from a settler to a friend back in Britain describing pioneer life;
   d) a drawing of one aspect of pioneer life;
   e) a report of what roles and work men and women performed in pioneer settlements;
   f) any other aspect of pioneer life which you would like to show. When your folder is complete, prepare a suitable cover for your material. Exchange your pioneer folder with another group.

3. Unrest in Upper and Lower Canada
(pages 294-297)

Can You Recall?
1. Identify and explain the following terms: a) Governor, b) Council, c) Elected Assembly, d) Château Clique, e) Family Compact
2. Make a diagram showing the relationship of the Governor, Council, and Elected Assembly. Explain why this relationship sometimes caused problems in the 1830s in Upper and Lower Canada.
3. Why were many people unhappy with the system of government in Lower Canada in the 1830s?
4. Why did each of the following make many settlers unhappy in Upper Canada?
   — system of land distribution, schools, church lands, absence of roads, Family Compact

Research
1. In Canada, we now have a system of responsible government.
   a) Find out more about how this works.
   b) What happens if the Prime Minister (or Premier) and cabinet do not have a majority in the House of Commons (or Assembly)? Has this ever happened?
2. Invite your Member of Parliament or of the provincial assembly to come to your class. Brainstorm with other members of your class to prepare questions about the work of our elected representatives.

Creative Experience — a Simulation in Making Decisions
Your class is planning a party. Have a class discussion using the following rules:
a) Each person must donate $1 for the funds.
b) The class may make decisions after taking a vote.
c) The teacher is in charge of the discussion. He/She does not have to listen to the wishes of the majority of the class.
d) The teacher shall choose a committee to run the party and spend the money. The class will *not* have any control over these decisions.
e) The teacher (governor) and the committee (council) can ignore the wishes of the majority of the class (assembly).

Carry out your class discussion and make your plans. How did you feel if the teacher ignored the wishes of the class? What did you want to do?

4. Rebellions of 1837 (pages 298-301)

5. Emergence of British Columbia (pages 302-305)

Can You Recall?

1. a) Describe what happened in the rebellion in Lower Canada in November-December 1837.
   b) Explain the ideas and the role played by Louis-Joseph Papineau. What happened to him?
2. a) Describe what happened in the rebellion at York in Upper Canada in December 1837.
   b) Explain the ideas of William Lyon Mackenzie. What happened to him?
3. Explain the two main recommendations of Lord Durham. How was each intended to end the conflict in the Canadas?

Ideas for Discussion

1. Form a small group of three or four students. Make a list of reasons
   a) why you think settlers should have supported the rebellion.
   b) why you think settlers should have opposed the rebellion.
   c) why you think that settlers should have supported reform but not the use of violence.
2. Write a report giving reasons for the rebellion of 1837 in Upper *or* Lower Canada. In your concluding paragraph, give your reasons for opposing or supporting the rebellion.

Be Creative

1. After further research on the topic, have a class debate: Resolved that we should support (or suppress) the rebellion of Mackenzie and Papineau.

Can You Recall?

Match the place in column A, with the description in column B.

A		*B*
a) Louisiana Purchase	i)	area west of the Rockies shared by Britain and the U.S.
b) Fort Langley	ii)	area in which gold was discovered in 1860
c) Oregon Country	iii)	land obtained by the U.S. from Napoleon
d) Cariboo District	iv)	British Crown colony established in 1858
e) British Columbia	v)	first British fur depot on the west coast

Ideas for Research

1. Write a researchy report on one of the following:
   a) James Douglas — the father of British Columbia
   b) the rush for gold in British Columbia

Be Creative

1. Do research on the growth of British Columbia up to the 1860s on one of the following topics:
   — Fort Langley
   — Fort Victoria
   — gold rush in the Cariboo
   — Barkerville

   Draw a picture to represent this place or event. Explain its importance in the development of British Columbia.
2. Do further research on James Douglas. With a partner, develop an interview. (You might include some of the following ideas in your interview — his background, his arrival in B.C., his attitude to the gold rush, his hopes for British Columbia, his achievements as Governor.) Present your interview to the class.

Units 1. The American Civil War as a Cause
of Confederation
2. Internal Factors Leading to
Confederation
3. Expansion from Sea to Sea
4. Metis Grievances, 1880
5. 1885: Triumph and Tragedy

1. The American Civil War as a
Cause of Confederation (pages 306-309)

Can You Recall?

1. Why did the 11 southern states wish to secede (separate) from the Union in 1861? How did this lead to the U.S. Civil War?
2. Explain how events during the Civil War led to hostility between the British and the Northern U.S. forces.
3. What were the Fenian Raids? How did they encourage the Confederation of the British North American colonies?

Ideas for Discussion and Research

1. The question of the right of part of a country to secede is a very complicated one. The issue still exists today.
   a) Did the southern states have the right to secede?
   b) Do states (or provinces) have that right today?
   c) Research one of these areas. Compare your answer with others in the class.
      (i) Quebec from Canada
      (ii) Pakistan from India (1940s)
      (iii) Palestinian peoples from Israel
   d) Is there any "right" answer to this question of secession?

Research

1. Do further research, and write a report on one of the following:
   a) the Underground Railway (the movement of escaped slaves from the United States to Canada)
   b) the ideas of Abraham Lincoln (include his background, his views on the preservation of the Union, his views on slavery, his importance as an American president)
   c) The Fenian raids on Canada, and their effects on helping to bring about Confederation.

Be Creative

1. In groups of four or five, prepare a "jackdaw" on the American Civil War. Include:
   a) a *map* showing the northern and southern states;
   b) a poster calling on support for the North or the South (or both);
   c) a description of a key battle in the Civil War (e.g., Gettysburg);
   d) a drawing of a northern or southern soldier (or both);
   e) a letter from a wife or mother during the war.

2. Internal Factors Leading to Confederation (pages 310-315)

Can You Recall?

1. How would each of the following factors have encouraged the colonies of British North America to join together in the 1860s?
   a) need for trade between colonies;
   b) desire to break the political deadlock in the Canadas;
   c) opinions of leaders, such as Macdonald, Cartier, and others.
2. Make a chart for the Charlottetown and Quebec conferences.
   Use the following headings as organizers: Location, Date, Colonies Represented, Decisions Reached

Research

1. Select one of the "fathers of Confederation" to study. In groups of two, research and write a report *or* prepare an interview on his views about Confederation. Your report or interview should include:
   - his background;
   - his reason for supporting Confederation.
   (You may research a "father of Confederation" from your province when it entered Confederation, if it was after the 1860s.)
2. In groups of two, prepare an interview with A.A. Dorion or Joseph Howe or one of the other opponents of Confederation. In your interview, as Dorion or Howe, explain why you are opposed to Confederation. State what your alternative proposal would be.

Creative Research — Group Activity

Prepare a newspaper, dated July 1, 1867.
In small groups of four to six, prepare a newspaper for July 1, 1867. Include in your newspaper some of the following:
   - pictures or drawings of Confederation events
   - pictures or drawings of some of the fathers (and mothers?) of Confederation
   - reports from the provinces
   - reports from other parts of British North America *not* in Confederation in 1867
   - reports from around the world in 1867
   - editorial cartoon
   - editorials
   - advertisements
   - notices of social events
   - reports on sporting events
and other items that interest you.

3. Expansion From Sea to Sea (pages 316-319)

Can You Recall?

1. a) What were the conditions of purchase of Rupert's Land from the Hudson's Bay Company in 1869?
   b) What advantages did this provide for Canada?
   c) What problems did it create?
2. Manitoba, 1870
   a) Why was there conflict between the Canadian government and the Red River colony in 1869?
   b) What was Louis Riel's role as leader at Red River?
   c) What were the final terms of admission of the new Province of Manitoba?
3. British Columbia, 1871
   What factors led to British Columbia joining Canada in 1871?
4. Prince Edward Island, 1873
   What were the conditions of admission of P.E.I. in 1873?

Research

1. Do research on the expansion of Canada. Select one province (perhaps your own) and research its entry into Confederation. Write a report to include:
   - conditions before entry
   - terms of entry
   - advantages and disadvantages for the province you study
     Select one of the following for your report:
   - Manitoba, 1870
   - British Columbia, 1871
   - Prince Edward Island, 1873
   - Saskatchewan and Alberta, 1905
   - Newfoundland, 1949
2. Class bulletin board display
   Each person should prepare a drawing, picture, or poster showing some aspect of the expansion of Canada. Create a display board, under the heading *Canada, from Sea unto Sea.*

4. Métis Grievances, 1880 (pages 320-323)

Can You Recall?

1. (a) Why was there a need for a police force in the West in the 1870s?
   (b) Explain how Macdonald formed the "red coats" (North West Mounted Police) in 1873.
2. Why did migration from Eastern Canada create problems for the Métis in the 1880s?
3. List the main grievances of the Métis in the Northwest in the 1880s.

Research

1. Select one of the following. Research the ideas and role played by this person in the Northwest in the 1880s.
   a) Louis Riel
   b) Gabriel Dumont
   c) Crowfoot
   d) Poundmaker
   e) Big Bear
   f) Sam Steele

   Write up your research in a 3-to-5 paragraph report.
2. Group Activity
   Prepare a "jackdaw" on the N.W.M.P. Your folder should include:
   a) a picture of a "mountie" (of the 1880s)
   b) a recruiting poster
   c) a letter from a mountie on duty in the Northwest
   d) a newspaper account of the role of the Mounties among the Natives and settlers

   When you have collected your material, prepare a suitable cover folder.
3. Picture Collection
   Draw a picture and describe one of the following:
   a) Red River cart
   b) "Prairie Schooner"
   c) Native travois
   d) prairie sod huts
4. Assign groups of students to research the grievances of the Métis and Native Peoples. Have a representative of each group present a petition describing the problems to a Court of Petition. Students should be assigned to speak as petitioners, or members of the Court. All other students should be reporters to write a newspaper account of the Court of Petitions.

5. 1885: Triumph and Tragedy (pages 324-329)

Can You Recall?

1. Describe at least five problems faced in building the transcontinental railway in the 1880s. Compare them with others named by your classmates.
2. Describe how the CPR was completed at Craigellachie on November 7, 1885.
3. How were troops moved by the CPR in spring 1885 to put down the Northwest Rebellion?
4. a) Why did the Métis finally resort to force in 1885?
   b) Describe briefly what happened at Batoche.
5. Why was Riel brought to trial? What were the results?

Ideas for Discussion

1. Why was the completion of the CPR considered a "triumph"? In small groups, list at least five advantages for Canada of having the transcontinental railway. Compare this list with the other class lists.
2. Why have many people considered the hanging of Louis Riel to be a "tragedy for Canada"?

Creative Research

1. In groups of four, create a "jackdaw" on the CPR. You should include:
   - map of the CPR in 1885, with the main centres located
   - a poster advertising for workers on the CPR
   - a letter (imaginary or real) from a worker
   - a drawing about building the CPR
   - a brief biography of one of the leaders in building the CPR
2. Do research on the trial of Louis Riel. Prepare to re-enact the trial. Individual students should be assigned to be:
   - Louis Riel
   - Riel's defence lawyers
   - the prosecutor
   - Gabriel Dumont
   - witnesses for Riel
   - witnesses against Riel
   - Chief Poundmaker
   - six jurors
   - the judge (your teacher)

All other members of the class will be newspaper reporters. They should write a report of the trial.

Glossary

aborigine   one of the earliest known inhabitants of a country

Acadia   the areas of French settlement and culture in the Maritime Provinces

adze   tool like an axe having a blade set across the end of the handle and curving inward

alliance   union of groups, societies, or nations for safety or a common purpose

ambassador   highest-ranking representative of one government to another

ancestor   person from whom one is descended; forerunner

Anglican   official church of England; a member of that church

anglophone   one whose main language is English

annexation   the addition to one's holdings, usually by force, of property or land, and usually of one country by another

anthropologist   one who studies the origin, development, and customs of humans

apprentice   a person learning a trade or skill on the job

archaeologist   one who studies ancient times by means of examining the remains of ancient cities, tools, buildings, graves, by digging and classifying those remains

architecture   science or art of building

artifact   anything made by human skill or work

artillery   the part of any army that manages big guns, such as cannons

artisan   a craftsperson; person skilled in some industry or trade

Asia Minor   peninsula of extreme western Asia between the Black and Mediterranean seas, comprising most of Turkey in Asia

assimilate   absorb, as a national or ethnic group by a larger group

astronomy   science that studies the planets, stars, and space

balance of power   an even distribution of military and economic power among nations or groups of nations

barter   trading goods for other goods without using money

Basque   a distinct group of people living in Northern Spain and in Southern France

Beringia   a land connection between Asia and Northern America in a period when the ocean had receded because of an ice age

bilingual   speaking two languages equally well

biological   about plant and animal life

blockade   the control of who goes in and out of a place by an army or navy

botanist   one who studies plant life

bribery   paying someone to act dishonestly or against the law for the benefit of the one paying

bronze   a mixture of copper and tin

bullion   lumps or bars of gold or silver

Bushmen   a South African tribe of people who lead a Stone Age way of life

Cabinet   the advisers of a prime minister or premier

campaign   series of actions planned to achieve some goal or to gain some possession

Canadien   name used to distinguish Canadians of French descent from the European French in early days of setlement; now the name for French Canadians

carbon-14   radioactive material that is used as a tracer in dating ancient material and artifacts

Cathay   name for China in the middle ages

censitaire   tenant of a seigneury

charter   a written grant to a colony, a group of citizens, a commerical company, or other institution

Château Clique   governor's council in Lower Canada in the early 19th century

chronology   system of putting events in order as they occurred in time

Cipangu   name of Japan in the middle ages

circumnavigate   to go around completely, as in sailing around the world

civilization   nation or people that have reached an advanced stage of social growth

civil war   a war between two groups of citizens of one nation

clergy   persons ordained for religious service: priests, pastors, rabbis, ministers, etc.

coalition   a temporary union of statesmen or states for some special purpose

communicate   pass along information by writing, talking, etc.

communism   a system characterized by government control and sharing of the economic resources of the community or country

compatriot   a person of one's own country

Confederate   referring to the southern states of the U.S.A. during the Civil War

confederacy   a union of states or countries

Congress   the U.S.A. lawmaking body, consisting of the Senate and the House of Representatives

conquistador   a Spanish conqueror in North or South America in the 16th century

conservation   preserving from harm, decay, or loss

conservatism   the tendency to keep things as they are; opposition to change

constitution   the system of basic principles according to which a nation, state, or group is governed

convent   a religious community, especially for nuns

convert   change from one religion, political party, etc. to another

creation   the making of the world and all things in it

Crusade   any one of the military expeditions between 1096 and 1272 to recover the Holy Land from the Moslems

cult   a system of religious worship

culture   customs, arts, way of life of a nation

customs (border)   the office at an entry point to a country where taxes are paid on things brought into the country

democracy   government that is run by the people who live under it

dialect   a variety of a language that differs from the standard language

dissent   differ in opinion; disagree about rules of a government or beliefs of a religious group

Dorset   an Inuit culture of Northeast Canada and North Greenland from about 100 A.D. to 1000 A.D., skilled in carving and hunting seal and caribou

dyke   bank of earth or a dam built as a defence against flooding by a river or the sea

economic   having to do with the managing of income, supplies, and expenses of a household, community, or government

empire   group of countries or states under one ruler or government

enclosure   wall or fence used to close off something, such as farmlands or pastures

environment   all the surrounding conditions and influences that affect the development of a living thing

epidemic   rapid spread of a disease

Eskimo (Inuit)   Native Peoples of northern Canada

ethnic   having to do with various cultural groups of people and their characteristics, language, and customs

expulsion   a forcing or driving out

evolution   *political* - growth and development of a system; *biological* - process of formation or growth; gradual development

factory (fur trade)   building where things are made; a trading post where furs were processed

Family Compact   governor's council in Upper Canada in the early 19th century

federal   having to do with a central government formed between provinces or states for handling common affairs

felting   making cloth by rolling and pressing together wool, fur, or hair for hats, slippers, and pads

fiord   a narrow inlet of the sea between high banks or cliffs

fishery   an area where fishing and processing of the fish is done

flake   a slatted platform used for drying fish

flesher   a tool for stripping the meat from the bones of an animal carcase

fleurs-de-lis   lily flowers, symbols of the French kings and of France, New France, and of Quebec

flint-knapping   skill of splitting hard quartz so that sharp projectiles (spearpoints and arrowheads) and knives, etc. are made

francophone   one whose main language is French

free trade   trade unrestricted by taxes, customs, duties, or differences of treatment

Gaelic   language of Gaels in Scotland or Ireland

genocide   systematic wiping out of a natural, cultural, religious, or racial group

geologist   one who studies the earth's crust, and its history

glacier   a large mass of ice formed from snow on high ground which moves slowly down a mountain or along a valley

guerrilla   member of a small independent group of fighters who harass the enemy by sudden raids, ambushes, etc.

habitant   settler in New France

habitation   dwelling or group of dwellings

habitat   place where an animal or plant naturally lives or grows

Helluland   Flat Stone Land, probably Baffin Island

hemisphere   half of the earth's surface - north, south, east, or west

heretical   holding a belief different from the accepted belief on one's church, school, or profession

heritage   what is or may be handed on to one from his or her ancestors

hieroglyph   picture of an object standing for the word, idea, or sound

Holy Land   the land where Jesus Christ lived and taught

Homo sapiens   human being; the species that includes all races of humankind

Huron   a tribe of Iroquois Indians living in Southern Ontario east of Georgian Bay

ice sheet   a broad, thick sheet of ice covering a very large area for a long time

76   **immigration**   a coming into a foreign country or region to live

immunity   resistance to disease

Indian (Native People)   the name given by Europeans to the majority of Native Peoples of North America

indulgence   forgiveness of the punishment still due for a sin, after the guilt has been forgiven

Industrial Revolution   the change from an agricultural to an industrial civilization, especially that which took place in England from around 1750 to around 1850

influenza (flu)   serious contagious disease

intendant   the most important officer in New France, responsible for finance and the day-to-day affairs of the colony

Inuit   a group of Native Peoples living in the Arctic region of Northern Canada

Iroquois   a group of Indians living mostly in the area near Lake Ontario and the St. Lawrence River

Islam   the Moslem religion

isolation   state of being set off or apart from others

kayak   Inuit canoe made of skins stretched over a frame of wood or bone

legend   a story coming down from the past, which has been widely accepted as true

league (distance)   about three or four kilometres

legacy   money or property left to one by someone else who has died

legislative council   a small group of officials appointed to advise the governor

legislature   group of persons who make the laws

Lent   in the Christian church, the 40 days before Easter, kept as a time of fasting and repenting of sins

linguist   one who specializes in the study of languages

Lower Canada   until 1841, the name for Quebec

Loyalist   one who remained loyal or faithful to the British government during the American Revolutionary War (1776-1783)

mammoth   an extinct member of the elephant family, extremely large, covered with hair, and having long, curved tusks

Markland   Forest Land, probably Labrador

mass   church service in Roman Catholic Church

massacre   wholesale, pitiless slaughter of people or animals

mastodon   an extinct animal that resembled an elephant

medieval   belonging to the Middle Ages, the period from about 500 A.D. to about 1450 A.D.

mercenary (soldier)   serving for pay in a foreign army

Métis   a person of mixed European and North American Indian ancestry

migration   movement of a large group of people or animals from one place to another

militia   a citizens' army; a reserve army

mission (settlement, etc.)   a religious outpost, usually used for missionary purposes

monastery   building where monks or nuns lived

monk   in the Christian church, a religious man who usually lives in a monastery

monopoly   exclusive control of a product

multicultural   usually of a society made up of many cultural groups, such as Canada's population

Muslim   Moslem, a follower of Mohammed and his religion

nationalism   patriotic feelings or efforts; often leading to a desire for national independence

Native Peoples   in Canada, the first peoples of the land, these include the Indian nations and the Inuit

navigator   a person who sails a ship or flies an aircraft

Neanderthal   early people widespread in Europe in the early Stone Age

Neolithic   of the later Stone Age, marked by settlements based on agriculture

nobility   the upper class, a class in society usually having hereditary title, rank, and power

non-conformist   one who refuses to follow the rules of an established church or authority

obsidian   hard, dark, glassy rock; volcanic rock, used by early humans for making tools, such as axes

Orient   the East; countries in Asia

origins   beginnings or source

outport   any of the isolated fishing villages along the coasts of Newfoundland

outpost   a settlement, village, or defence post away from the main population or army

pagan   person who is not a Christian, Jew, or Moslem

patent   an exclusive right given to a person or group to produce a product

patriation   to bring something to the country for which it is meant, such as a national constitution

Patriot (American)   one of the early members of the revolutionary movement in the thirteen colonies fighting for independence from Britain

Patriote   one of the French-Canadian reformers in Quebec in the 1830s

pemmican   dried, lean buffalo or venison meat pounded into a paste used by fur traders and explorers in the West and North

petition   a formal request to a government or superior in authority

pictograph   picture used as a sign or symbol, used in some kinds of writing

pigmentation   colouring matter in tissues of living things

pilgrimage   journey to some sacred place as an act of religious devotion

plantation   a large estate or farm, especially in a tropical or semitropical country, on which cotton, tobacco, sugar, etc. are grown

pope   supreme head of the Roman Catholic Church

portage   carrying of boats, canoes, provisions, overland from one stretch of water to another

pound   enclosure for keeping or trapping herds of wild or tame animals

prairie   a large area of level or rolling land with grass but few trees, as in the central plain of North America

pre-Columbian   events of the time before Christopher Columbus sailed to the Western Hemisphere

press-gang   in former times, a group of men whose job it was to obtain men, by force, for service in the army or navy

prospector   a person who examines a region or area for gold, silver, oil, etc.

Protestant   a member of certain churches formed after the break with the Roman Catholic Church in the 16th century

provisional government   a temporary government set up until a permanent one can be established

pueblo   an Indian village built of clay and stone dwellings (southwest U.S.A.)

purgatory   in Roman Catholic belief, a temporary condition or place in which the souls of those who have died penitent are purified from sin or the effects of sin by punishment

Puritan   in the 16th and 17th centuries, a group in the Church of England that wanted simple forms of worship and stricter morals

pygmy   a very small person, such as groups that live in Africa and Asia, one of various Negroid people of equatorial Africa

pyramid   a tomb or temple having a square base and triangular sides, built by ancient Egyptians

quintal   a unit of 100 pounds (about 50 kg)

race   one of the major divisions of humankind having certain physical qualities in common

radical   in politics, favouring fundamental changes in the social or economic structure

radioactive   giving off radiant energy in the form of rays

rations   fixed allowances of food; daily allowances of food per day for a person or animal

Reformation   16th-century movement to reform the Roman Catholic Church but which ended by forming new and protestant churches

régime   a system of government or rule

registered (Indian)   a recorded Indian, given special status and rights by the British and Canadian governments

Renaissance   a great revival of art, literature, and learning in Europe in the 14th, 15th, and 16th centuries

representative government   a system of government in which laws are made by the elected representatives of the people

republic   a nation or state in which the citizens *elect* representatives to manage the government, the head of which is a president rather than a monarch

responsible government   system of government in which the cabinet or executive is responsible to the elected representatives of the people

revolution   a complete change or overthrow of government, or in the way things are done

sachem   a North American hereditary chief

saga   a type of prose story of heroic deeds written in Iceland or Norway in the Middle Ages

scurvy   a disease characterized by bleeding gums, and weakness, caused by the absence of vitamin C from the diet

secede   withdraw formally from an organization, especially from a political organization, such as a nation of states or provinces

sedition   speech or action causing rebellion against the government

seigneury   a tract of land granted to an individual by the King of France

shaman   a priest or medicine man among Native Peoples tribes

skraelings   Native People that the Vikings saw in Labrador and Newfoundland

smallpox   a disease that brings fevers and causes blisterlike eruptions to the skin; sometimes fatal

sovereignty   the supreme power of the state belonging to the people of that state

speculators   people who buy land, property, or commodities for resale usually at higher prices

squadron   a group of ships, planes, soldiers that is part of a larger group

steerage   part of a passenger ship occupied by those travelling at the cheapest rate, usually below deck

stratigraphy study that deals with the order and make-up of layers of deposit of soil, rock, and objects within those layers

symbiosis the association or living together of two unlike organisms for the benefit of each other

symbol something that stands for, or represents an idea

tariff tax charged by a government for goods coming into the country

technology inventions or machinery used to improve building or manufacturing

theologian a person skilled in the study of God and religion

Thule an Eskimo culture of North Greenland, lasting from about 500 A.D. to about 1400 A.D.

tolerance willingness to allow others their beliefs and differing ways of life

treason betrayal of one's country or ruler by helping the enemy

tribe a group united by race or custom within a larger group (the nation)

tuberculosis infectious disease usually affecting the lungs

tundra a vast, level, treeless plain in the Arctic regions

typhus acute infectious disease characterized by high fever, skin eruptions, and weakness

umiak large, flat-bottomed boat with a wooden frame covered with skins and used by the Inuit

Union the Northern States in the American Civil War (1861 - 1865)

Upper Canada until 1841, the name for Ontario

Vatican papal palace in Vatican City in Rome, the centre of the Roman Catholic Church

viceroy a person ruling as the deputy of the monarch

Viking one of the groups of Norsemen who raided the coasts of Europe during the eighth, ninth, and tenth centuries A.D.

Vinland an area probably in the Maritime area of Canada, visited by the Vikings about 1000 A.D.

voyageurs boatmen in the service of the early fur-trading companies

War Hawk nickname given to settlers of the middle United States in the 1800s, who wanted to urge war against Canada

web of life the belief that all things are connected and dependent upon each other.